THE
EARLIEST ENGLISH

LIVING & DYING IN
EARLY ANGLO-SAXON
ENGLAND

For museum curators,
an endangered species?

THE
EARLIEST ENGLISH

LIVING & DYING IN
EARLY ANGLO-SAXON
ENGLAND

Samantha
Glasswell

TEMPUS

First published 2002

PUBLISHED IN THE UNITED KINGDOM BY:
Tempus Publishing Ltd
The Mill, Brimscombe Port
Stroud, Gloucestershire GL5 2QG

PUBLISHED IN THE UNITED STATES OF AMERICA BY:
Tempus Publishing Inc.
2 Cumberland Street
Charleston, SC 29401

British Library Cataloguing in Publication Data.
A catalogue record for this book is available from the British Library.

ISBN 0 7524 2534 X

Typesetting and origination by Tempus Publishing.
Printed in Great Britain by Midway Colour Print, Wiltshire

Contents

List of illustrations

Text figures

Colour plates

Acknowledgements

Writing this book has been a team effort. My long suffering husband, Kim Glasswell, provided perpetual moral and practical support, particularly in caring for our son, David. However, he also had the courage to read the text and tell me when he thought I had got things wrong!

As I can neither draw, nor wield a camera, there would be few illustrations without Richard Knox's drawing and Manda Kemp's photographs. Both had to work in less than ideal conditions and with problematic subject matter. I am also grateful for the considerable moral support. Special thanks are also due to Dr Richard Underwood for the location map and Sahra Mallard (my talented sister-in-law) for two of the reconstruction drawings.

Several specialists have also provided assistance. Dr Jenny Wakely read and commented on 'In sickness and in health', thereby enhancing it significantly. Steve Houghton read and discussed sections on farming, despite the interference of a most dramatic thunderstorm. It is also nice to know that breaking his collarbone was not for nothing. Helen Hollingsworth's farming experience was also of great help. I am particularly indebted to Alan Baxter of West Stow Anglo-Saxon Village, not only for lengthy discussions but also for kind permission to use images taken at the site. If you have not been, West Stow is well worth a visit. Neil Finn of the University of Leicester Archaeological Services gave me access to material from Eye Kettleby and discussed the site at length. Richard Knox and Peter Liddle of Leicestershire Museums, Arts and Records Service provided background information on many of the smaller Leicestershire sites. Mary Hider read much of the text and unravelled my spelling. As a scientist, her comments made me re-evaluate many statements and theories. Heather Southorn, of Leicester City Museum Service, advised on artefact decay and conservation. My brothers, Gary and Michael Middleton, and my sister Lesley Elliot have fielded questions about metalworking and nursing respectively. A big thank you is owed to Dave Elliot for saving my disks when the computer died on me.

John Lucas, Curator of LCMS Jewry Wall Museum, must have thought I had moved in. His patience in providing me with access to the collections and the indispensable library will not be forgotten. Richard Clarke, Oriane Genol and Anita Harrison, all of Jewry Wall, assisted me in many ways including providing tea and pencils. LCMS also gave permission for the reproduction of reconstruction drawings by Mike Codd. Robert Moore of Northampton

Museum kindly supplied information and Tim Clough of Rutland County Museum gave permission to photograph objects from his collection. Anglian Water also generously allowed material in their ownership to be illustrated.

Members of Wulfingas AD 450 Society, especially Jane Hillyard, Stuart Reid, Matt Cooper, Danny Seager, Richard Knox, Manda Kemp and Kim Glasswell, have been of great help, posing for photographs and discussing ideas.

Thanks must also go to my mum and my much missed dad for encouraging my passion for archaeology and for never trying to persuade me to do something sensible. Finally, I would like to thank Karen Dixon for believing I could do this and starting the whole adventure off. I hope I have not let you down.

All mistakes, over-simplifications and omissions remain my responsibility.

1 Introduction: exits and arrivals

Who is this for?

In many ways, the early Anglo-Saxon period is the 'Cinderella' of British archaeology. It is sandwiched between the beautifully civilised, terribly clever Romans and the rough but rather exciting Vikings. Consequently, our Anglo-Saxon forebears have often been overlooked or disregarded. Ironically, at their height, the earliest English produced objects as exquisite as the finest Roman mosaic and at their worst were probably as savage as any Viking marauder.

This book aims to explore the world of the Anglo-Saxon warriors and settlers who came to England during the fifth and sixth centuries AD. It is not an exhaustive study but a starting place or a summary. The period covered begins with the arrival of the Anglo-Saxons and finishes approximately with the coming of Christianity. It is hoped that this introduction will be of use to re-enactors, primary school teachers and anyone interested in the diverse and fascinating origins of the English.

Troubled times, the end of Roman Britain

Britain in Roman times contained many elements which would be familiar today. A significant number of people lived in towns and cities with markets, shops and public buildings such as bathhouses. Although it was ruled by Emperors whose dominions stretched as far away as Africa, there was also a place for local government in the form of town councils. The countryside was dotted with farms, many being estates with comfortable villas decorated with mosaic floors and painted wall plaster. The provinces of Britain were protected by a professional standing army. A network of roads provided good communications for the soldier and the merchant alike. Certain goods, such as pottery, were mass-produced and exotic items were imported from across the Empire. Christianity came to Britain during this period but pagan religions continued to be followed. However, life was far from perfect and even for the comfortably rich there was trouble ahead (1).

1 *Late Roman buckle and strap end from Leicester.* Photograph by A. Kemp, courtesy of Jewry Wall Museum, Leicester

Change and uncertainty can be uncomfortable to live through but fascinating to study. The transition from Roman Britain to Anglo-Saxon England was just such an era. Usually things change gradually. The ending of Roman Britain was no exception. Possibly from as early as the third century AD, Saxons began to carry out raids on the provinces of Britain. By the fourth century, there were also problems with the Scotti from Ireland and Picts from Scotland. The Roman military responded to this, in part by the construction of forts around the East Anglian and South coasts, known today as the Saxon Shore Forts. However, a string of events weakened the position of the Britons. During the last years of the fourth century, a Roman general of Spanish origin, Magnus Maximus, carried out campaigns in Britain against the Picts and Scots. On their successful completion he declared himself Emperor in AD 383. However, the Romans already had an Emperor and Magnus left Britain to pursue his claim, taking some of the army with him. Magnus' bid for power failed and he never returned. By the end of the fourth century, Britain was again under attack from the north and a general called Stilicho was sent by Rome. Stilicho also fought successfully but left Britain in AD 401-2. Other areas of the empire were also in danger and Stilicho took contingents of British soldiers with him to reinforce his command. In AD 407, Britain was under threat of Germanic invasion so a British leader, Constantine, took an army to Gaul to head it off. He was not successful and a serious barbarian attack occurred. At this point the British people lost patience with Imperial administration, rebelled against the Emperor, and drove off the barbarians themselves (Johnson, S. 1980).

As new coinage had been brought to the province primarily to pay the army, this dried up. However, it did not mean the use of coinage stopped because old issues could remain in circulation for a considerable period. Coins in use today can be 30 years old. Mass production of pottery in Britain also ceased. Pottery seems to have continued to be made on a smaller, more local scale for a significant period of time, but with few changes in style. These factors do not mean that the Roman way of life ceased, but they do mean that archaeologists have very little to date post- or sub-Roman sites. For example, around this time there is evidence of prolonged activity at Binchester Fort in County Durham with buildings being subdivided, then changing from dwellings to workshops, but there is very little to indicate exactly when these changes were taking place.

Documentary evidence for this time is thin. The Greek historian Zosimus records that in AD 410 the Emperor Honorius told the cities of Britain to 'look to their own defence'. It is interesting that the letter is addressed to the cities, not to any particular Imperial official. This has led some to suggest that Honorius was carrying out a face-saving move rather than abandoning Britain. As described above, the Britons had already expelled Roman officials and broken away from Imperial control. Whatever the truth of the matter, AD 410 is usually regarded as the end of Britain's inclusion in the Roman Empire.

Contact was still maintained with mainland Europe and the Christian faith was still practised. In AD 429, Bishop Germanus visited Britain and led the people in battle against the Saxons and the Picts. This success became known as the Alleluia Victory and was recorded by the Briton, Gildas, who was possibly a monk writing some time before AD 547.

Around the middle of the fifth century, raids by Saxons became too much for some Britons and they migrated to Gaul, perhaps in groups organised by the Christian church, which still maintained international connections. Some settled in Armorica, known today as Brittany and later still, others left for Spain. Where there had once been Roman provinces, small kingdoms seem to have developed.

The arrival of the Anglo-Saxons

With insufficient troops for the defence of Britain, alternative strategies had to be developed. Fire would be fought with fire. Germanic peoples were brought to Britain as mercenaries and were given land in return for military service against other 'barbarian' raiders. An account of this was recorded by an Anglo-Saxon but not until a couple of centuries after the event. In his *Ecclesiastical History*, the Venerable Bede records that people were invited to settle by the British King or Proud Tyrant, Vortigern. However, after a time, the mercenaries decided that the land was good and the Britons weak so they sent word home for more people to join them and they rebelled against the Britons. Bede relates that the settlers included Saxons from what is now Northern Germany, Angles from southern Denmark and Jutes from Jutland in Denmark.

Many battles now ensued as Briton and Anglo-Saxon fought for control of the land. It was a time of heroes, including Ambrosius Aurelianus who rallied the British resistance. The Britons' greatest victory was at the Battle of Mons Badonicus or Mount Badon, which is supposed to have halted Anglo-Saxon expansion for fifty years. This is the backdrop for the legends of King Arthur, long before castles and knights in shining armour. But British heroes and occasional victories were not enough to send the invaders back over the sea.

The Anglo-Saxons did not carry all before them, with western areas including Wales and Cornwall remaining largely British. However, in the Midlands and the East, Germanic settlement continued. Eventually, the former provinces of Britannia became the Anglo-Saxon kingdoms of Mercia, Lindsey, Wessex, Essex, Sussex, East Anglia, Diera and Bernicia (later Northumbria) and Kent. Traditionally, the Angles settled in Norfolk, Suffolk, the Midlands and the North East, the Saxons in the South and the Jutes in the Isle of Wight and Kent. The reality was probably somewhat more complex.

Who were the earliest English?

By the mid-fifth century, eastern Britain was becoming a very racially mixed and diverse area. It is not known how many Germanic warriors and settlers were involved. Some scholars have argued for mass migrations with the British population being driven away, killed or enslaved. Others suggest that a Germanic elite took control but the Britons remained under new masters. However, it is possible that the situation varied from area to area. At the end of formal Roman rule, Britain was not one province but at least four. Some suffered more at the hands of raiders than others and so their response is also likely to have differed. The Anglo-Saxon mercenaries and

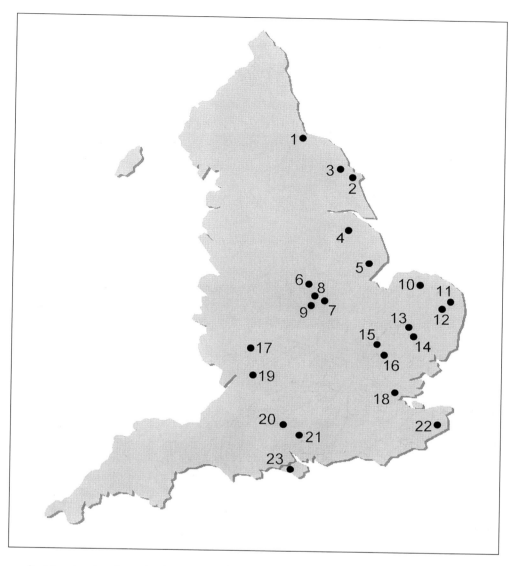

2 Map showing the main sites mentioned in the text. Produced by R. Underwood
1. Norton, Cleveland 2. Sewerby, Yorkshire 3. West Heslerton, Yorkshire
4. Fonaby, Lincolnshire 5. Tattershall Thorpe, Lincolnshire 6. Broughton Lodge,
Nottinghamshire 7. Empingham, Rutland 8. Eye Kettleby, Leicestershire
9. Thurmaston, Leicestershire 10. Spong Hill, Norfolk 11. Caistor-by-Norwich,
Norfolk 12. Morning Thorpe, Norfolk 13. West Stow, Suffolk 14. Westgarth
Gardens, Suffolk 15. Edix Hill, Cambridgeshire 16. Great Chesterford, Essex
17. Beckford, Hereford and Worcester 18. Mucking, Essex 19. Lechlade,
Gloucestershire 20. Portway, Andover, Hampshire 21. Alton, Hampshire
22. Buckland, Dover, Kent 23. Chessell Down, Isle of Wight

settlers were also not one nation. Bede mentions Angles, Saxons and Jutes, but other peoples including the Franks and the Frisians are likely to have been present.

The fate of a whole region could pivot around a charismatic leader like Ambrosius but often even crucial individuals can disappear into the mists of time. Whether one sees King Arthur as pure myth or military genius, it is probably no accident that this is the time in which his legends are set. In some areas, the newcomers may have integrated with the Britons and adopted their customs. At the other extreme, Germanic settlers may have driven out or murdered the existing population. Anglo-Saxon societies were based around a warrior elite and the weapons found so commonly in their burials were not just for show. It is also possible that in parts of eastern England the Britons survived in substantial communities, only later becoming absorbed by the surrounding settlers.

So, it can be seen that the earliest English under discussion here are not merely Angle and Saxon mercenaries and their descendants. The terms 'English' and 'Anglo-Saxon' are used here for ease but it must be remembered that this was a multicultural society. A person may be buried in an Anglo-Saxon manner, accompanied by a full range of Anglo-Saxon possessions, but she may still have been able to trace her ancestors back through hundreds of years of Roman rule in the provinces of Britannia.

Finding out

A history of the English settlements as described above, can be pieced together from fragments of documents that have survived for hundreds of years, but there is another method of learning about this time and these people. Archaeology is the study of peoples' pasts through their material remains: the pottery they made; the jewellery they wore; the crops they grew; the weapons they fought with; traces of the structures they built and the cemeteries where they buried their dead. Much of the information in this book is based on a series of sites stretching from the north-east of England to the Isle of Wight (**2**). All have been published as archaeological site reports and can be followed up in more detail should the reader so wish (see bibliography). Each site offers a different slant on the period and its people. Had other sites been selected then the details of this work would probably have been different, but hopefully, not the general conclusions. Archaeology is a powerful and detailed method of looking at a past people. It can be used to examine the technology, wealth and complexity of a society.

However, there is one major limitation that must be remembered. Archaeology can seldom, if ever, tell us what a person thought or believed when they were making or using the artefacts and structures that are found today. The archaeologist has to interpret the finds and try to deduce what motivated people in the past. Individual archaeologists can have alternative interpretations and sometimes they will make mistakes. However, this is not a drawback, but is what makes it all so exciting. There is still much to discover.

Archaeology tells us that the Anglo-Saxons arrived because objects are found which are very different from the Roman period that came before. Cemeteries, with skeletons accompanied by many objects, or pots containing burnt human bone are found. Roman buildings with stone walls give way to hollows in the ground and holes where posts once stood, all that now remains of Anglo-Saxon timber houses. Metal detectorists find fragments of highly decorated, even gaudy brooches, but the days of Roman painted wall plaster and decorated mosaic floors are well and truly gone.

2 Death and burial

Much of what we know about the earliest Anglo-Saxons comes from how, and with what, they buried their dead. Burial practices display wide-ranging variations, but without the benefit of written sources it is very difficult to know what these meant. There are two main forms of burial that we know the Anglo-Saxons used. The body was either buried (inhumed) or burnt (cremated). There are other ways of disposing of the dead that leave little or no archaeological trace, such as river burial. Whether or not the Anglo-Saxons also used such rites is a matter of guesswork.

Burying the body

There are many inhumation and cremation cemeteries dating from the fifth to the seventh centuries which provide a great deal of information about the people buried in them. The shape and size of the graves, the bodies themselves and objects which the living chose to give to the dead all have a story to tell (**colour plate 1**). When attempting to understand the earliest English, it is often possible to collect large quantities of data but converting this to meaningful insights into lifestyles and beliefs is a more taxing and frustrating exercise. Despite the many uncertainties, looking at how graves were made and cemeteries organised may yield clues about the communities who created them.

Making the grave

The shape of graves shows great variety. At West Heslerton most graves were ovate but rectangular ones with rounded corners were favoured at Buckland. Burial pits could be irregular (**3**), or even square or circular as seen at Norton. Grave floors were flat, uneven or scooped. Sometimes, a deliberate effort was made to support the head of the body with a raised earthen pillow. A similar feature was discovered in the grave of a woman at Easington in County Durham where a concentration of small pebbles acted as a cradle for the head. Some graves were made with great skill, having steep and even sides, but others, even in the same cemetery, appear to have been roughly dug. On some occasions the gravedigger struck a problem and in one particular

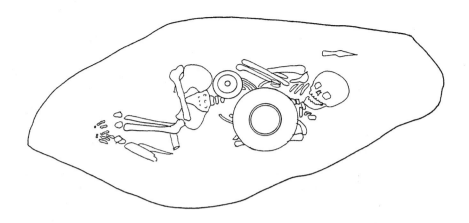

3 *There was no standard grave shape; this example at Empingham II is irregular.* Redrawn by R. Knox

example at Buckland, the tool used for digging must have broken. Archaeologists found it still embedded in the graveside.

It is likely that most cemeteries would not have been busy enough to support a full-time gravedigger and the contrasting quality of workmanship may simply reflect the deceased's family doing their best. However, for a people used to digging pits, trenches and so forth, preparing a neat and regular grave should not have been too arduous. A poorly-cut grave does not necessarily indicate a lack of respect for the dead person, although in some cases it could be an explanation.

In most archaeological excavations, the modern ground surface is not the same as in Anglo-Saxon times. Today's level can be higher or lower so it is difficult to know how deep the grave was originally. Observations do show that there was no uniform depth for burials. Certain cemeteries have a tendency for infants and children to be buried more shallowly but adults are also found at the same depth. In some cases, deep graves contain the most objects. Grave size similarly displays no strict standardisation. Large examples can be over 3m (10ft) long, while the smallest are just large enough to hold a baby.

Graves were not always simply pits in the ground. At Lechlade, one burial structure is referred to as a 'family vault' because it was lined with stone and contained five people. Ledges are sometimes found in the gravesides, which appear to have supported a plank ceiling and at Empingham II some skeletons were disturbed when the planks rotted and the roof of the grave caved in. High ledges were recorded at Buckland, but in one child's grave the ledge was too low for a body to have been placed beneath it. In this case, perhaps a false floor was made to put the body on. Flints were discovered at the same cemetery that had been deliberately brought to some graves and placed in a number of arrangements, including along the sides of the burial and completely covering it.

This great diversity in form implies that there were no specific, limiting 'rules' relating to grave construction. Any shape and dimension that would accommodate the body and its grave goods seems to have been acceptable.

The physical process of burying a body in a cemetery, even a short distance away from the home, means that the corpse had to be transported. In twenty-first century Britain, a coffin is usually used for this and the deceased is protected from view. The rituals that accompanied the last journey of an early Anglo-Saxon can now only be guessed at, although the poem *Beowulf* describes two funerals with mourners and women singing dirges. In more recent years, millions of people watched the funeral procession of Diana, Princess of Wales, her coffin mounted on a gun carriage with princes walking in its wake, symbols of national mourning, yet surmounted by a floral tribute which said simply 'Mummy'. However, this most elaborate procession and passage of the dead left no record that would be identifiable using archaeology, Diana's actual grave being relatively simple and many miles away from where her funeral took place.

There is evidence that the earliest English also used coffins, although their ceremonies are lost. Soil stains occasionally survive in the ground, formed as the planks decayed and at West Heslerton, a fragment of oak was preserved above the body. When all traces of wood have disappeared metal fittings such as bolts, joining strips and corner pieces indicate the presence of coffins. These are not common because Anglo-Saxon woodworking skills were such that metal was not an essential material in coffin construction. This makes it difficult to estimate how frequently coffins were used. There is some evidence for alternative arrangements such as a stretcher-like bier. Again at Buckland one grave had its corners extended, seemingly to allow the interment of the body and bier together.

Positioning the body

Most people were laid in the grave on their backs. Their arms were placed in a range of positions including by their sides, or across their waist, pelvis or chest. Their legs could be straight, or crossed at the ankle or calf. Burial in this manner lends itself to displaying grave goods because many, especially those belonging to women, were worn on the front of the clothes. Alternatively, individuals were often laid out on their sides facing either to the right or left. This can give the appearance of someone curled up asleep and in some cases the person may have died whilst sleeping and have been buried before the effects of rigor mortis had worn off. There are instances where a bed was placed in the grave with the owner still on it. Very tightly curled positions, referred to as crouched, are also found but are less common. At Lechlade, one person was even found in a sitting position. Some skeletons can be found in strange poses that are the result of bones being moved by the processes of decay of the soft tissue.

A small percentage of burials are found face down, or prone. Although this is not common it is seen in numerous cemeteries but particularly in the north. Prone interments include men but are slightly more common among women. Despite being face down, many of these burials have been laid out with care and possessions have been placed in the grave. However, in some instances the body appears in a disturbingly contorted pose. One explanation could be that the corpse was accidentally dropped and, rather than climb into the grave to lay it out again, those present have filled the pit in. If disrespect was intended, the body may have been deliberately thrown into its grave. Conversely, it has been argued that these people were buried alive and the twisted nature of their torsos and limbs are the result of trying to push themselves up and out of the ground. Sites where this has been suggested are as far apart as Kent and Yorkshire.

Live burial would not necessarily be deliberate because some medical conditions, such as deep comas, would have been indistinguishable from death with the knowledge available at the time. The possibility remains that on some exceptional occasions people were forced into graves and buried while they were still obviously alive. It is difficult to imagine this as anything other than a punishment for a heinous crime. In Tacitus' history of the early Germans, he records that the punishment for adultery was death by drowning and burial in a bog. However, if live burials occurred when people were so abhorrent to their society that a horrific execution was required, why were they allowed to remain part of the community in death, buried among their friends and families? At Sutton Hoo in Suffolk, there is a royal cemetery with its famous seventh-century ship burial, but there is also a group of later, Christian period interments that seem to be execution victims. In death, they are set apart from those they knew in life.

Most graves contain the remains of one individual but it is not uncommon to find two, three or more people together. An adult with a baby is a frequent combination that in many cases is probably a mother and child. However, at Empingham II, infants were also buried with adult men and in one grave three children were buried together. It is still likely that these people were related and died around the same time. This is not surprising if the cause of death were an infectious illness such as diarrhoea, causing chronic dehydration, which might kill members of a family in rapid succession. Other multiple burials contain people who did not die at the same time, but the grave was reopened for further bodies to be added. At Lechlade, in one instance, a significant time had elapsed after the first burial because its defleshed bones were disturbed when a second interment took place. Multiple burials were not restricted to inhumations. The cremation cemetery at Spong Hill produced evidence for pits being reopened to allow more urns to be added. These cases represent the deliberate association of people after death, even to the extent of returning to an exact plot to bury individuals together who had died years apart. Kinship was vitally important to the earliest English. Relatives lived and worked together, protected and cared for each other, so it seems reasonable to argue that these burials are family groups.

Archaeologists have occasionally found pupal cases on objects associated with the body. These are likely to come from insects feeding off the corpse and so indicate that decay had begun before the body was interred. This has led to the argument that graves were left open to view for a period so that the body was visible for mourners not able to attend the funeral. However, leaving a body in an open grave for display has certain logistical problems. Wild animals and birds would attempt to feed on it and a permanent guard would be necessary to prevent this. In some periods, particularly the Neolithic, people's remains were deliberately left exposed so that the flesh would be removed, but this leaves traces on the bones, usually teeth marks. The writer knows of no such evidence on Anglo-Saxon skeletons.

Open graves can collapse, under certain circumstances, and some soil types would be more prone to this than others. Shoring up the gravesides would be required, at least in some areas and at particularly wet times of year. Therefore, a body left at the mercy of nature is unlikely to be viewed at its best even after a relatively short time. But people do feel a need to see that a dead loved one is at peace. An alternative would have been to lay the body in state in a building where at least it would be safe from the elements and some carrion feeders. This could be a dwelling or another one of the buildings found on a settlement. The objects could still be placed around the person, and friends and family would have a chance to pay their last respects. Similar practices were carried out within living memory. My mother remembers having her grandmother's body laid out in the front room of her home. Displaying bodies inside buildings would not prevent the onset of decomposition and the creation of pupal cases on artefacts nearby. A different possibility is that a person died away from the settlement and the body was not discovered until decomposition had begun.

Grave markers and burial mounds

Graves were sometimes dug into or through earlier ones in a manner that suggests that no trace of the first interment was visible above ground. However, this is relatively rare suggesting that a long-lasting marker was used to show the location of a burial at the surface. This is proved by the fact that graves could be deliberately reopened to allow another individual to be added to a family group. A low mound of soil would be created by the burial but additional markers may have been incorporated. No gravestones have been found from the earliest period. Stone is a very valuable building material and tends to be reused in later structures, but even allowing for this recycling at least a few should have survived if they were originally used, as is the case with Roman tombstones. Wood was the material used extensively by the early Anglo-Saxons and graves could have been marked with posts or plaques, perhaps carved to identify the person or family buried there. Eventually, these would rot away. Piles of stone, like the flints mentioned above from Buckland, could have been used to create a cairn (stone mound).

Cremations, as well as inhumations, were marked and in some instances the methods employed could be elaborate. At Alton, grave seven was a cremation of an adult and an infant in a round pit. Post holes and small slot trenches in the soil showed where a rectangular structure had stood over the pit. As well as a post at each corner the slots suggest it had walls made of vertical planks (**4**).

Perhaps the most dramatic method of marking the location of an interment was to cover it with a vast earthen mound or barrow. The time, labour and extra land required for such a monument means that they were restricted to the privileged few. The mound covering the ship at Sutton Hoo is likely to be dedicated to a king or perhaps a high king (bretwalda, literally meaning

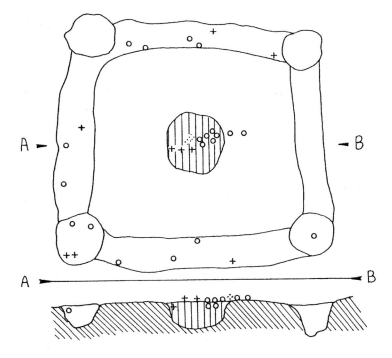

4 *Cremation seven at Alton, Hampshire is a covered, square structure with a post at each corner. Redrawn by R. Knox from Evison*

ruler of Britain). If a person was not quite important enough for his or her own barrow, then the next best thing was to be situated adjacent to or inserted into someone else's, usually towards the edge and not with the first burial in the centre. Barrows did not have to be Anglo-Saxon in origin and Bronze Age barrows, already over a thousand years old, were adopted for secondary burials. In other cases, prehistoric barrows are used as a focal point or a boundary for a cemetery.

Why was it important to so visibly mark the location of high status burials? The main period of Anglo-Saxon barrow building was in the seventh century, which was a time of change when kingdoms were developing, fighting for their own survival, and attempting to dominate others. Raising burial mounds was costly in terms of resources and in itself demonstrated power. Barrows altered the landscape and made a physical connection with it. Burying the ruling elite in this way manifestly staked a claim to a place, the dead and the land became one. Using man-made features, which were already ancient, associated the present with the past and asserted a concept of belonging and inheritance. This helped to legitimise the claim to authority over that area and the people who lived there.

Possessions for the dead

If a cemetery is discovered unexpectedly it is usually very easy to tell if it belongs to the early Anglo-Saxon period. This is due to the practice of burying things with the dead. Although this occurs during other eras, the range of material included with Anglo-Saxon burials is both extensive and distinctive. Categories include dress fastenings and accessories, weapons, grooming equipment and tools.

It is vital to remember that archaeologists only recover a selection of what was originally included in the burial. Materials such as fur, textiles, wood and leather will leave only traces if they survive at all. Depending on the type of soil, the body and bones of the person may disappear completely, leaving only tooth enamel and a stain on the soil.

Although some items are found with both men and women, the type of things buried with a person seems closely related to their sex. However, this has come into question recently because it is now common practice to determine an individual's gender by examining their bones and in some cases this has been found to be at odds with what the grave goods imply. This has led to the argument for transvestite men and warrior women. Although it is known that some women played a vital military role, such as Aethelfleada, King Alfred's daughter, these theories must be scrutinised before they are accepted.

The number of cases where the conflict of gender exists is relatively small. The reliability of sexing using bones depends on which ones are available for study and although a particular part of the pelvis is 95 per cent accurate there still remains a margin for error. Today's society is more tolerant of alternative lifestyles and there is a danger of reading this back into a more prejudiced time. Initial DNA studies of material found recently seem to support the mixing of grave goods and gender but skeletons from older excavations may not be suitable for examination using these techniques because they may have been exposed to contamination. More conclusive answers may come in the near future from further material collected in stringent, scientific conditions.

Certain classes of artefact do cross the boundaries of gender. Many of these are connected with the preparation and consumption of food and drink. Pottery vessels such as cups, jars and bowls are relatively common finds and occur with men, women and children. Similar items made from wood must also have been common. Although such vessels would not survive, wood has a tendency to split, especially if used for containing liquid. As turning a wooden item on a lathe is a very time-consuming process, splits were often repaired using metal sheets. In some cases, rims and embellishments of copper alloy and silver were also part of the original object. These metal components do survive and sometimes preserve traces of the wood they were originally attached to. Many species were used including wild cherry, ash, chestnut, maple and beech. The metal fittings could be very plain and simple but also decorative and elaborate. A pair of wooden cups from a woman's grave at Buckland had silver rims that were attached with silver strips decorated with birds' heads. At Westgarth Gardens, a wooden bowl with an embossed copper alloy band riveted on below the rim accompanied a woman. The angle of the band suggests the vessel was of rounded, perhaps globular shape (**5**). Such objects would have been works of skill and beauty so it is not surprising that most surviving examples come from reasonably wealthy graves.

5 *A wooden bowl from Westgarth Gardens was adorned with a decorative metal band (rim diameter 11.5cm).* Redrawn by R. Knox from West

6 *Reconstruction drawing of copper alloy bowls for cooking and serving food.* Drawn by R. Knox

Glasses for drinking from were a luxury. A variety of types survive. Cone shaped beakers accompanied both rich men and women. A more unusual type from Westgarth Gardens is more cylindrical with a broad base but has lugs on the rim perhaps for suspension or to hold a glass handle that was lost or broken before burial. Perhaps the most dramatic type of glass used by the Anglo-Saxons was the claw beaker. This has a basic cone shape but has hollow glass claws added in rows around the central section. Claw beakers were probably inspired by Roman glassware and originate on the continent, but types found in England date from the fifth century onwards. The number of claws and the colour of glass change through time. Blue-green, green and brown were common during the fifth and sixth centuries but in the seventh century new colours including emerald green and royal blue were introduced (**colour plate 2**). Most examples found in England were probably imported from Belgium but there is good evidence that there was a maker in Kent. Glass vessels in the shape of drinking horns are found on mainland Europe but are extremely rare in England. Two were discovered near Rainham in Essex during sand and gravel digging in 1937. Again, they were probably imported from Belgium in the seventh century but their dating is uncertain.

Copper alloy bowls and cauldrons were probably used for warming or serving food. Some have lugs, which would have allowed them to be suspended, but others have a foot ring and probably held pride of place on the table during a banquet (**6**). Such items are usually found with adults but do occur with children. Most copper alloy bowls were imported from the continent, thus heightening their value.

Miniature buckets were buried with wealthy men, women and children. These were made of wooden staves, yew having been identified in some examples, bound together with vertical and horizontal copper alloy bands, riveted through the wood. The rim was formed from a copper alloy sheet.

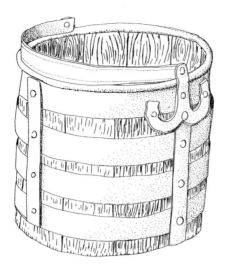

7 *Reconstruction drawing of a miniature bucket. Some examples have decorated copper alloy bindings (10cm high).* Drawn by R. Knox

8 *Reconstruction drawing of a large, iron bound bucket (19cm high).* Drawn by R. Knox

9 *Knives were an essential everyday tool for women, men and children (blade lengths varied from 5-14cm).* Drawn by R. Knox

The metal bindings and handle were often decorated with punch designs (**7**). Miniature buckets are very decorative but what practical function they fulfilled, if any, is unclear. They may not have been watertight because rivets pierced the staves and wooden buckets usually need to be kept wet to stop the wood shrinking and creating gaps between the individual components. More functional buckets did occur in rich graves, but tend to date from the late sixth century onwards, the period when grave goods were becoming less common. As well as being larger, these buckets have staves bound with iron bands that would have been put on while hot. As the iron cooled it contracted and drew the wooden components tightly together (**8**).

What do these objects mean? Perhaps the early Anglo-Saxons needed banqueting equipment fit for the halls of the gods and this is what the wealthy were provided with: beautiful vessels made of glass, metal and decorated wood. Those of lower rank would have equivalents in plain wood and pottery. However, the richly furnished graves belonged to those people who in life were symbolically responsible for providing for those below them. They would be expected to give banquets that bound society together with ties of obligation. This role may have been represented after death by the vessels interred in their graves.

In contrast, knives are one of the most common finds and occur with men, women and children (**9**). If there is only one artefact in a grave it is often a knife. They were an essential everyday tool but were relatively small, often around the size of a modern fruit knife. At some sites, size seems to have been generally influenced by age and gender, children having the smallest, women having those in the middle range and men tending to have larger knives, but there was much overlap between the categories. Knives were carried around, usually on the waist belt, supporting the idea that they were used for many purposes throughout the day, not just for eating. At Empingham II, the position of a small number of knives in graves has led to the suggestion that they were strapped to an arm or leg. The blades were made of iron but this is brittle and will shatter, which in turn makes it difficult to work into a sharp edge. To overcome such problems, many knives incorporate small amounts of steel as a core, or added to the edge, or the sides and tip of the blade. The steel could be sharpened and, when the edge dulled, re-sharpened. Blades composed of iron alone would require constant sharpening, but never with as good a result. Traces of leather on blades show that knives were kept in a sheath that was decorated in some cases. At Buckland, lines were observed on some sheaths and one may have been open-work leather, lined with a coarse fabric. Sturdier sheaths were made of wood covered in leather. Knife handles were commonly made of horn, but wood was also used.

Some items found with both men and women are associated with grooming and appearance. Combs of bone and antler are found in many inhumation cemeteries, but in small numbers. Double- and single-sided types were used. Single-sided combs can have a relatively straight back, or can be

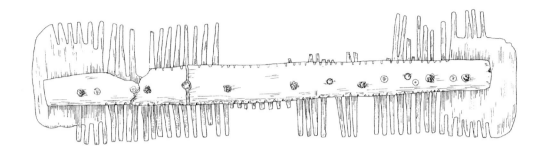

10 *Double-sided bone comb from Leicestershire (14cm long).* Drawn by R. Knox, courtesy of Leicestershire Museums Arts and Records Service

curved or triangular. Double-sided examples were made with plates of teeth, held together by a central rib or bar. This joining piece often has many fine saw cuts along its edges which show that the teeth were cut into the bone or antler plates after the comb had been assembled (**10**). The early English did not forego an opportunity for decoration and combs are frequently adorned with ring and dot motifs.

Tweezers were made of iron or copper alloy. Iron ones tend to be plain but copper alloy versions show a range of decorative embellishments including incised lines and punch marks (**11**). They could have been used for a range of purposes. Thorns and splinters must have been an everyday irritant for a people living so close to nature. However, removing unwanted hair is a further possible use but it has been suggested that women may sometimes have used tweezers for getting an extra grip on a needle if sewing a particu-

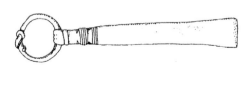

11 *Tweezers, like these from Leicestershire, are found with both men and women.* Drawn by R. Knox

larly difficult material. Experiments have shown that this works very well. Although thimbles were used in Roman and Medieval times, the writer knows of no Anglo-Saxon examples.

Men, and less often women, were occasionally buried with a particular type of purse which had an iron bar with a buckle attached to it. These bars could be bowed or straight but with curved or spiral ends. It is thought that the bar was fixed to the front flap of the purse and was used in conjunction with, for example, flint or iron pyrites, as a strike-a-light (**12**). The buckle allowed the pouch to be carried on a belt, but easily removed when it was needed for starting a fire. Textile and leather found adhering to the iron are probably the remains of the purse. This in itself may have been used for holding tinder.

Women's burial, in all their finery

Women's graves produce a number of objects that seem to have been worn, either as dress fastenings or accessories. Metal objects survive relatively well and there can be an abundance of these in female graves. Brooches are a common find until the last part of the sixth century when they become less frequent. Brooches come in diverse shapes and sizes, but are grouped into a number of categories (**colour plate 3**). They can be made of iron, copper alloy, silver and gold. Some are very simple and plain, but others are elaborately cast with animal motifs or encrusted with garnets. The exact types found generally depend on where in the country the woman was buried.

Clasps were used on sleeves in the Midlands, Norfolk, Suffolk and the North East. These too show great variation in shape and decoration and changed over time. Numerous other items are found such as pins, buckles and strap ends, which were all used on clothes. Ivory rings from purses represent another type of functional object, as do combs. Cosmetic scoops and brushes suggest that early Anglo-Saxon women may not have been devoid of vanity. Others objects appear to be merely decorative, such as the many glass and amber beads. However, these may have carried deeper

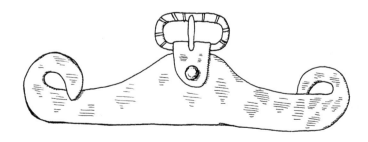

12 *Metal purse mounts acted as strike-a-lights (10.5cm long).* Drawn by R. Knox

13 *Spindle whorls from Leicestershire made from (left to right) bone, clay and reused pottery fragment. The pin beater below was also used in textile production.* Photograph by A. Kemp, courtesy of Jewry Wall Museum, Leicester

meanings for the people at the time. Some artefacts are now more difficult to understand and could have symbolised status, or have been kept for protection against bad luck.

Graves also contain objects connected with working life. Spindle whorls were weights from drop spindles, which were used for spinning wool and flax into thread for weaving and sewing (**13**). Whorls were made from numerous materials including pottery, chalk and bone, some of which were decorated. Even rich women were buried with their spindles but in some cases their whorls were made from beautifully facetted transparent crystals. On rare occasions, a wealthy woman was buried with an iron weaving batten. This resembled a blunt sword and was used to beat the threads closer together as they were woven on a loom.

The types of grave goods found change over time. Many classes disappear altogether, but a few new ones appear. Wooden boxes with iron fittings tend to date from the later sixth century onwards and are found with wealthy women. It is possible that in earlier times boxes with no metal parts were also buried with the dead but have left no trace. Surviving examples tend to be rectangular, hinged and with a handle on the lid. Other iron plates formed locking mechanisms consisting of a bolt on the inside of the box, which could be released with a simple key.

Small cylindrical, metal boxes appear after Christian missionaries had arrived in England. These boxes usually had one removable end and were suspended from a chain. They are thought to be needlework boxes and scraps of cloth and pins have been discovered inside them (**14**). However, some of them appear to be decorated with a Christian cross and this has lead to the suggestion that they belonged to converts to the new faith and may have held items of religious importance.

No one grave would contain all the objects mentioned above. Archaeologists find graves rich in artefacts but there are also graves that have only a knife or no grave goods at all.

Men's burial

A man's burial tells us a lot less about what he wore. Belt buckles are the only common finds connected with costume. Very rarely, a circular brooch may be found, perhaps for a cloak.

Weapons for warriors

Weapons are the main type of find from male graves indicating certain features of life at that time. Anglo-Saxon society had a great potential for violence. The process of settlement was probably peaceful in some cases and in some

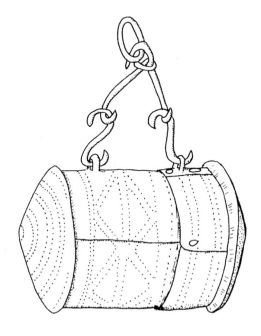

14 *Reconstruction drawing of a needlework box (6cm long).* Drawn by R. Knox

15 *Well-armed warriors both bearing a spear and shield, and one also carries a sword.*
Photograph by A. Kemp

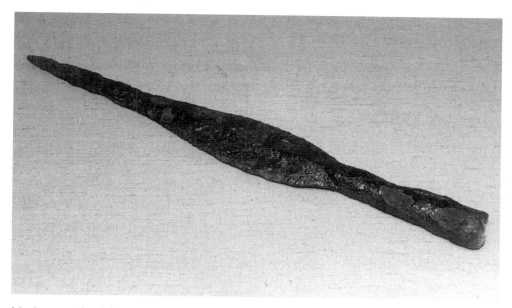

16 *Iron spearhead from Leicester.* Photograph by A. Kemp, courtesy of Jewry Wall Museum, Leicester

areas. However, in many instances, the Anglo-Saxons took the land from the existing British population by force. Once the Anglo-Saxon kingdoms were established, they fought amongst themselves. Later came Viking raiders followed by Viking armies. Eventually, Anglo-Saxon rule was ended with their defeat by the Normans at the Battle of Hastings in 1066. In addition to large-scale conflict, in a society with no police force or prisons, there is also the potential for violent encounters with outlaws or brigands (**15**).

Anglo-Saxon society was a warrior society. The spear is the most common weapon found in graves. It had a symbolic as well as a practical purpose and a later law code states that only a free man could possess a spear. A slave was not even permitted to carry one and the punishment, if caught, was to have it broken across his back. As a spear shaft would not break easily, this represents a severe beating. Status was not dependant on age and spears are regularly, if infrequently, found with young children, but they tend to be small examples. They also occur with men whose long-term medical condition would have rendered them unable to fight. This reinforces the impression that spears were more than just functional weapons.

Spears vary greatly in shape and size (**16**). Some have rounded outlines and are referred to as leaf shaped but others are angular. Parallel-sided examples, reminiscent of a modern kitchen spatula, are also found. In cross section, they can be oval, diamond or even stepped. Different categories gain and lose popularity over time but as with all similar metalwork, each item was individually handmade, so strict standardisation should not be expected. Almost all share common features: they were sharp, pointed and would kill an opponent if thrust into his face, chest or stomach with sufficient force. Later, Anglo-Saxon poems suggest that spearheads may sometimes have been smeared with poison.

Spearheads had a socket as well as a blade that allowed them to be firmly attached to a wooden shaft. A long rivet through the socket and shaft ensured the join was secure. Alternatively, a very small percentage of spearheads had a tang (a rectangular cross-sectioned spike), which inserted into the wooden shaft and may have been glued and bound to ensure a secure fit. Traces of wood survive in contact with the iron spearhead, showing that a number of different types were used for the shaft including hazel, poplar, alder birch, willow and ash. Such woods can be made to grow in long straight poles. In addition, the wood needed to be supple so that it could absorb the blows of other weapons without snapping. The range of species is interesting, perhaps reflecting what was both suitable and readily available. In poetry, Anglo-Saxon spears are usually referred to as being of ash.

Certain spear types had special uses. The angon had a long, thin rod of iron between the blade section of the head and the socket. This design would enable the spearhead to go right through the enemy's shield, rendering it useless and, if you were lucky, actually hitting the person behind the shield at the same time. Spears may have been used for hunting and general protection against wild animals. Specific forms could have been suited to such purposes.

The butt of the spear was frequently, but not always, encased in an iron cone called a ferrule. This could simply have allowed the warrior to stick his spear in the ground when not in use, but if it was broken in battle the ferrule was pointed enough to fight with. Where a ferrule and a spearhead both occur in alignment in the grave this can allow the total length of the weapon to be estimated. Again there seems to be no strict uniformity, most being between six and eight feet in length. However, some archaeologists have noted a general tendency for longer spears to be found with older men. At Norton, the longest spear was deposited with the oldest man.

In many instances, the spearhead and the ferrule are discovered pointing in the same direction, or very close together. This means the spear was broken before being placed in the grave. If the break was accidental, a spearhead could be removed from a broken shaft and attached to a new one or melted down as scrap to reuse the iron. The fact that this was not carried out suggests that the broken spear had some significance. It may have been deliberately snapped but it is not known why this was done. It could be a ritual 'killing' of the object that would be reborn in the afterlife with its owner. More prosaically, spears may have been broken to fit into the grave more easily.

Spears usually lie at the side of the body but their position can vary. At Empingham II, some seem to have been placed diagonally across the body, resting in the warrior's hands. In a limited number of cases, pins have been found near spearheads that may have been fastening a cover or wrapping.

17 *Shields had a handle in the centre covered with an iron boss which protected the warrior's hand (diameter 18cm).* Drawn by R. Knox

Shields were the next most common component in the early Anglo-Saxon arsenal, according to grave deposits. They probably belonged to men of a higher level of society. Shields were the warrior's main form of protection. Body armour, such as mail, is found exceptionally rarely. Shields comprised of a round board with a hole and a handle in the middle that was covered by a protective iron boss. This changes shape over time, with later examples tending to be taller (**17**). It is the boss and metal components of the grip that usually survive, but organic remains can be preserved in the metal's corrosion products. The shield board was made of wood, and fragments adhering to the boss rivets show this could be willow, poplar, alder, beech, maple or lime. In poetry, linden (lime) is the material usually referred to. The wood was covered with leather on the front and sometimes on the back as well. This would increase the strength and durability of the shield. Rivets indicate that the thickness of the board ranged from about 6mm to 11mm.

The handle was made separately of wood and metal. There were various methods of enhancing the ease and comfort of the grip. Twine or leather was wrapped around some, while textile woven tape was used on others. A layer of padding could be incorporated underneath. At Edix Hill, hair and feathers served this purpose.

Although they had a practical purpose, shields could be decorated with metal plates. Simple circular studs, abstract shapes and zoomorphic images were all employed (**18**). Sometimes, the rivets on the shield boss and circular appliqués were covered with silver, but in other instances, more elaborate embellishments with animal decoration and gilding also appear, as on a shield from Empingham II. The mounts gathered from Sheffield's Hill near Scunthorpe prove that even decorated shields were not just for display. Diamond-shaped holes from spear blows can still clearly be seen piercing the appliqués.

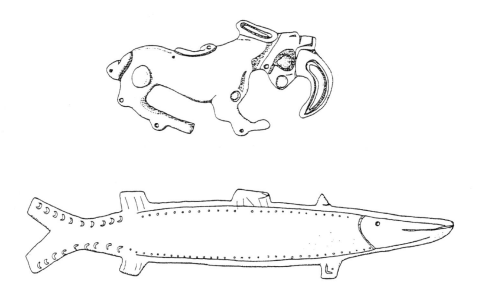

18 *Shields were sometimes decorated with metal appliqués like these from Bergh Apton and Morning Thorpe (top appliqué 4.8cm long).* Redrawn by R. Knox from Green, Rogerson and White

How big were early Anglo-Saxon shields? Researchers have measured the distance between appliqués and grave widths to obtain estimates. Heinrich Härke suggests that the average minimum diameter for shields is 35 to 50cm. Stains found in graves at Mucking suggest that most fell within a 60 to 64cm diameter. There is reason to believe that not all shields were put into graves complete. Shield studs are found in graves with no sign of the much more substantial boss. This implies that caution should be exercised in other instances where interment of an incomplete shield may be less obvious.

When considering shield size it is important to understand how they were used. Warfare tended to be based on groups of warriors facing each other in opposing lines (shield walls) (**19**). Spears were the main weapon and were thrust at the enemy standing directly in front but also at adversaries to the left and right. Therefore, a warrior had to defend himself from blows coming from several directions at once. This meant that a shield needed to be of a sufficient size to protect the combatant from the attacks he saw coming and the ones he could not (**20**). A shield of 64cm in diameter would cover a person almost from shoulder to knee and provide good protection of the torso and therefore the major organs. A shield significantly smaller might not create a big enough defensive barrier. However, there remains the possibility that different sized shields were needed for other purposes. Smaller shields would be advantageous for skirmishing in restricted terrain such as undergrowth or woodland. Shields were predominantly for defence but could be used offen-

19 *Warriors fought side-by-side with their shields forming a wall to protect them from their enemies' spears.* Photograph by A. Kemp

20 *With spear blows coming from all directions, it was vital for warriors not to step forward beyond their own shield line.* Photograph by A. Kemp

sively to punch into the face of an opponent or to slam against his body and knock him off balance. These tactics were probably used in single combat because in the shield wall they would leave the warrior too exposed to multiple spear blows.

Swords are found much less commonly than shields but the number varies greatly from cemetery to cemetery. Buckland produced 17 from 171 burials but this site was in use over a long period and the frequency of swords increased over time. Empingham II contained over 130 burials, but no swords while Westgarth Gardens had only 69 interments but two swords. North Luffenham in Rutland yielded ten examples, but the cemetery was discovered in the nineteenth century and the number of burials uncovered is unknown. Probably only the very rich or members of a high ranking lord's retinue possessed swords, which accounts for their rarity, but in addition there is evidence to suggest that swords were passed on as heirlooms, a practice mentioned several times in *Beowulf*. Archaeology supports this. At Buckland, one sword was found with a pommel probably made in the early sixth century. This was modified by the addition of a ring (see below) after the middle of the century, but the sword was not buried until the late sixth or early seventh century. Therefore, it could have been in use for a hundred years and passed through several generations before finally being interred.

Anglo-Saxon swords had long, broad iron blades that were diamond or lens shape in cross-section and were sharp along both edges. The end was pointed and sharp, but the sword was more suited to slashing than stabbing. Blades occasionally had a broad central groove called a fuller. As well as being forged, swords could be pattern welded, a skilled and time consuming technique in which rods were twisted then welded together and used for the central section of the blade. The result preserved the pattern of the twisted rods producing, for example, a herringbone or chevron effect thus making an impressive weapon even more dramatic or even magical. Could this be the inspiration for swords with special powers, like Excalibur? Pattern-welded swords are more common in Kent than elsewhere in England, and some were probably imported. Blades could be decorated by other methods, including the use of an inlay of another metal of contrasting colour. Another sword from Buckland had a ring inlaid on the blade surface, which was identified when the object was X-rayed. Such decoration may originally have been more common than can now be ascertained. This is because iron is very vulnerable once it has been removed from the ground and will deteriorate rapidly. The surface blisters and disintegrates thus destroying details like shallow inlaid embellishments. Keeping the artefact in special, dry storage conditions, ideally at 10 per cent relative humidity, can prevent this. Alternatively, professional conservators can clean and stabilise objects to enable them to survive in less ideal environments. However, such treatments are expensive and usually reserved for items on display in museums. Conservators are also reluctant to carry out procedures which cannot be reversed and tend to leave sections of an object

21 *In the early days of conservation, objects were stripped to a metal core thus destroying surface features and their original form.* Photograph by A. Kemp, courtesy of Jewry Wall Museum

with all the corrosion products intact and available for future study. This is because much has been learnt from the mistakes of the past when 'conservation' consisted of stripping off all concretions until a surviving metal core was uncovered (**21**). This resulted in swords and spearheads which resembled paper doilies because, ironically, it is the corrosion that preserves the original form and surface details of the object (**colour plate 4**).

The construction of the handle or hilt of the sword changed over time (**22**). Swords of the fifth century tended to have a handgrip and upper and lower guards made of wood, bone or horn. In the sixth century, large pommels of iron, copper alloy or silver and gold were introduced. The guards could still be made of wood, horn, bone or even ivory but were sandwiched between metal plates. In Kent, small, decorative rings were attached to the upper guard of the hilt of some swords. In earlier examples, this is a true ring that moved freely through the staple, which attached it to the sword, but later on, the ring and staple are made together as a solid piece. Their purpose is unknown, but they may have been used for making vows on. Lords are often referred to as the giver of rings so perhaps this is a gift from the warrior's master. Sword rings and hilts in general were often embellished with a variety of designs.

Swords may have been carried in times of security as a symbol of rank but they also retained their functional purpose as a weapon. A number of Anglo-Saxon skeletons have been found with sword wounds. As described above,

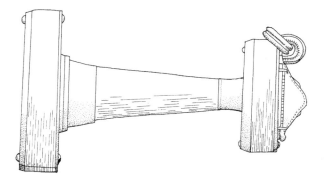

22 *Reconstruction drawing of a sword hilt with ring.* Drawn by R. Knox

warriors fought in lines with spears. Here the sword had limited use because spears were long enough to keep a swordsman at bay. However, if the lines broke up and one warrior with a spear faced another with a sword, the advantage was firmly with the latter. It would be relatively easy for the swordsman to knock the spear aside or close in on his opponent and use his sword to deliver a serious, if not fatal, slashing or stabbing blow. Sword against sword was an even match and some disputes or conflicts may have been settled

23 *Chape in the form of a man's head from the tip of a scabbard (3.8cm long). This type is usually described as Frankish but this example is from Leicestershire.* Drawn by R. Knox, courtesy of Leicestershire Museums, Arts and Records Service

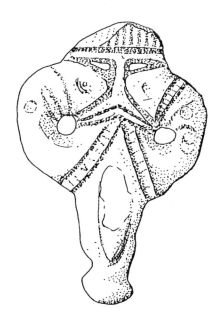
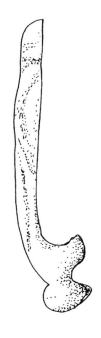

in single combat. Early Anglo-Saxon swords were heavy and unsophisticated, so although a warrior's skill was crucial, brute strength and stamina would be distinctly useful.

Anglo-Saxon swords were kept and worn in a scabbard made of wood and covered in leather. The leather may have been decorated. The scabbard mouth was often re-enforced because this would take the most strain when the sword was drawn or replaced. In some instances, twisted cords were bound around the top of the scabbard, but metal bindings of iron, copper alloy or silver along the edges were another alternative. Although serving a practical purpose, these were also decorative and could be made with imitation ribbing as well as being plain. The end of the scabbard could be protected with a metal cover known as a chape (**23**). Some scabbards were lined with fleece or fur, their natural oils helping to stop the sword from rusting and making it easier to draw. Swords were worn on belts or on a strap slung across the body known as a baldric.

Other weapons are found in graves but much more rarely. Throwing axes called franciscas are known. One grave from Empingham I cemetery in Rutland was very unusual because it contained twelve arrowheads of various shapes and sizes. Bows and arrows were probably used in hunting as well as in warfare (**24**).

Poor relatives?

There are a substantial number of male graves that contain no weaponry. Does this mean these people were all either slaves or very poor? Not necessarily. There are hints that men may have had other roles that precluded them from carrying weapons. This seems to have been the case with pagan priests, according to Bede. Men were occasionally buried with musical instruments but, apart from kingly interments, their burials do not include weapons as well. There may have been other circumstances where a man's position or occupation did not need to be represented in the grave, but these individuals could still have been significant and prosperous. This is a case where the surviving evidence is insufficient for us to be sure.

Babies and children

Mortality amongst babies was high and still more children who survived their early years died before reaching adulthood. Many juvenile graves are unfurnished but a significant number of children were buried with grave goods.

Frequently, only a single object is found with a child such as a pot, a pin, a bead or a knife. Other burials contain just a few artefacts but occasionally well-furnished examples occur. At West Heslerton, a two to five-year-old was

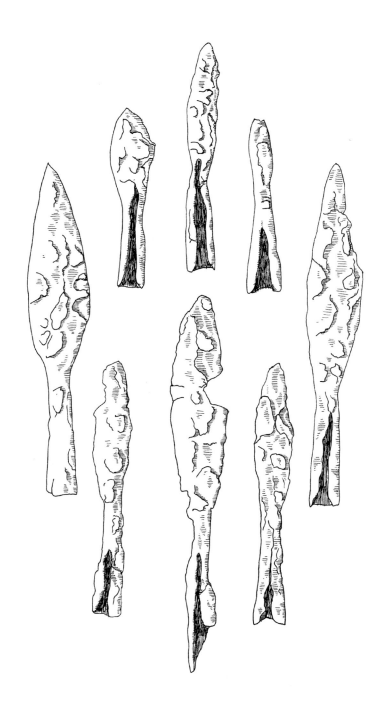

24 *Arrowheads from a grave at Empingham*. Drawn by R. Knox,
courtesy of Rutland County Museum

provided with annular brooches, a necklet, a knife, a pottery vessel, a dress pin and two beads. A child aged between seven and eight at Great Chesterford was interred with a spearhead, a shield boss, a knife and a dog, perhaps a pet. There are also cases where babies were given spearheads that they obviously could not have used. In these cases, young children were given the accoutrements of adulthood and status that suggests they were of a social rank that had to be symbolically displayed in death. This position must have been inherited, probably through ties of kinship, because these individuals were too young to have earned a place in society through their own merit.

Very few items seem to be specifically associated with children, although spearheads found with juveniles tend to be small. Possible exceptions are metal necklets that are found only rarely but would be more practical and safer than beads for a small child (**25**). At Sewerby, one child's grave contained two small brooches, which is unusual because most jewellery found with juveniles is of a size appropriate to adult use.

Young babies could be accompanied by grave goods and at Great Chesterford an iron pin was found with an infant under two months old while two glass beads were interred with another who was under four months old. Foetuses, probably either late miscarriages or stillborn babies, do have items associated with them but these are difficult to interpret and may not have been deliberately deposited in the graves. However, enough evidence survives to imply that as soon as a person was born they were an accepted member of society and had a recognised place within the community.

When did children become adults? Can the presence of certain grave goods give an indication? These are very difficult questions to answer. It is not normally possible to deduce exactly how old a person was when they died, but a probable range is usually suggested. Girls and boys may have been regarded as adults at different ages but before the late teens it is difficult to tell the genders apart by skeletal remains. Not all mature adults were provided

25 *Necklets, like this one from Empingham, are usually found with children.* Redrawn by R. Knox from Timby

with objects in their burial so the presence of grave goods in itself does not confer adult status. On the contrary, as seen above, some young children were sent to their grave with objects indistinguishable from older members of the community. However, taking into account the evidence from a great number of burials it can be suggested that around the ages of 12 to 14 many more young people are interred in graves settings that look like those of adults. Whether this is an accurate representation of a rite of passage in life remains a matter of speculation.

Through the pyre, cremation burials

The Anglo-Saxons also burned (cremated) their dead. This practice arrived with the settlers in the fifth century and continued into the seventh century. It may have ceased due to the influence of the new religion, Christianity, which taught that on judgement day the dead would physically rise up from their graves. An intact body was therefore a distinct advantage.

It may seem relatively easy to put a body on a bonfire and burn it, but cremation is actually a lot more complex. Anyone who has seen a relative's ashes scattered will know that modern cremated remains are a very fine powder. Anglo-Saxon cremations are quite different. As well as ash, relatively large and recognisable fragments of bone survive the burning. In fact it is quite difficult to burn a human body and a temperature of at least 40°C must be attained (McKinley, J. 1994). Wood was required to build and fuel the pyre and it has been calculated that 146kg of pinewood was needed (Holck, P. 1986). However, in parts of the world where cremation is still carried out on a pyre today, such as India, two or three times that amount is actually used. Fire will only burn as long as there is enough oxygen. Ashes from parts of the pyre that have already burnt could smother flames and embers, cut down oxygen supply and so start to put the pyre out. If a large object was put on the body, such as a shield, it would also deprive the body of oxygen and prevent it from burning properly. However, when a certain temperature was reached the body fats themselves began to ignite and these in turn would cremate the rest of the flesh, muscles and bones.

Observations at a modern crematory showed that women cremate more easily than men because they have heavier and different deposits of fat, but the very old and the young tend to be harder to cremate because they have fewer fat deposits. In Anglo-Saxon cremations the trunk, or torso, of the body burnt almost completely because this had the most fat, creating the highest temperatures, but the extremities, such as lower legs, feet and hands, will not have burnt as thoroughly (McKinley, J. 1994). In a cremation from the cemetery at Millgate, Nottinghamshire a wrist clasp, part of sleeve cuff, showed no sign of burning perhaps because a sufficient temperature was not reached in that part of the pyre due to the limited quantity of fat on a wrist.

Burning body fat also explains the modern myth of 'spontaneous human combustion'. In these cases people have been found dead but with parts of their corpses reduced to ashes while the rest of the body and clothes have not been touched by fire at all. Early investigators thought that somehow the person had burst into flames. In fact, the individual had usually died and come into contact with a heat source, such as a gas fire, which ignited an area of their body fat. The poor person has then burnt like a self-basting turkey. Pictures of these victims show vividly how easy it would be for an Anglo-Saxon cremation to contain parts of the body reduced to ashes alongside other parts that were dramatically less affected by the fire.

As can be seen from the above, to cremate a body successfully was a task fraught with difficulties. A method of pyre construction was developed which allowed the inclusion of sufficient fuel, maximised oxygen flow and helped deal with ash. Large timbers were built up in crossing layers and the gaps in-between were filled with brushwood (**26**). This ensured oxygen reached the centre of the pyre. In addition, the pyre could be built over a shallow pit, which would also have helped the air to flow particularly in the

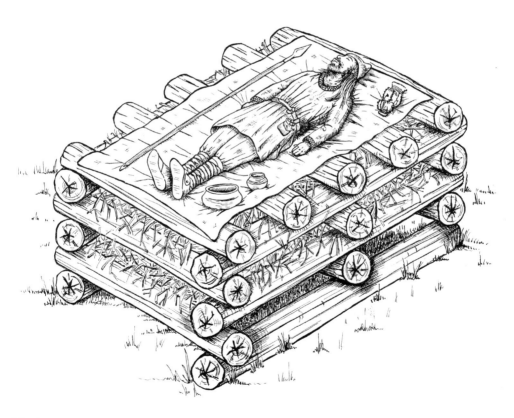

26 *Artist's impression of a cremation pyre. Weapons are found only rarely in cremation urns but may have been included on the pyre. Drawn by S. Mallard*

27 *Cremation urns from Thurmaston, Leicestershire.* Photograph by A. Kemp, courtesy of Jewry Wall Museum, Leicester

early stages. Later the pit filled with ash, which also might have ensured that unburned timbers were kept exposed to air. The site of a pyre would not usually survive to be discovered by the modern archaeologist but there are clues from the cremation urns at Spong Hill that the Anglo-Saxons used this method. Charcoal was discovered in 131 cremations coming from both larger timbers and brushwood. These fragments are probably the remains of the pyre. Oak, ash, pine, hazel and hawthorn groups were found. As some woods give off more heat than others the types may have been carefully selected. Modern pyre cremations in India take about three hours to complete (McKinley, J. 1994).

When the pyre had cooled or been dowsed with water, ashes were gathered, put in a pot and buried (**27**). Some cremation urns had pottery lids. A number of these were found at Spong Hill. Other pots may have had a leather, fabric or wooden cover, but these would have rotted away leaving no trace. Some pots do not contain human remains at all but only animal bone and ash (Hills, C. 1977). Occasionally, cremations are found without an urn and may have been held in a bag or a box. In some cases, there may have been too much ash for one pot and the excess was poured directly into the grave pit, or the remains of one person were divided between two urns (Hills, C. and Penn, K. 1981). The surviving bone fragments show that the remains of more than one individual were sometimes placed in the same urn. These people may have been related. Children and babies were cremated as well as adults. Urns came in many sizes and the smaller examples are often found to contain a child's remains.

Taking it with you

Grave goods were included in urns. At the cemetery at Caistor by Norwich, (Myres, J. N. L. and Green, B. 1973) about half of the 155 cremation urns contained objects, but caution is needed when studying these. If the site of the pyre was used more than once, possessions from one person may have been left behind, but later included with the ashes of a different person. This could be particularly important if something belonging to a woman ended up being buried with a man.

A great variety of grave goods are found such as brooches, beads, spindle whorls, glass vessels, buckles, wrist clasps and ivory bag rings. These are comparable with grave goods found with inhumations. However, bone combs, gaming pieces, tweezers, razors and small shears (comparable in size to nail scissors) are fairly common in cremations but are rarer in inhumations (**28**).

Some of the grave goods show signs of burning. At Spong Hill and Millgate, similar items such as brooches; glass beads and vessels; ivory and antler rings and spindle whorls were burnt. Tweezers, shears, razors and combs seem unburnt at Spong Hill and there is a similar picture at Millgate. However, items made of iron such as shears and razors are less likely to be affected by burning (**29**). The types of objects that are clearly burnt are those that were actually worn, such as brooches and beads. This suggests that in general bodies were cremated fully clothed.

Objects not worn, such as combs, were still put in the pot but may not have been on the funeral pyre. However, as McKinley (1994) points out there may be another explanation for the objects that seem unburnt. As described above, an Anglo-Saxon funeral pyre would not burn at the same temperature in all places. The part of the pyre around the body would burn with the greatest heat. The edges of the pyre would burn at a lower temperature and less completely. Therefore, objects that show no evidence of burning may have been on the edges of the pyre. As it is always the same types of objects which show no signs of burning there may have been an order for where

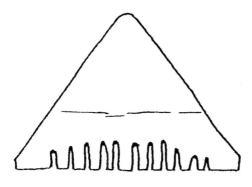

28 *Miniature comb of a type found in cremations.* Redrawn by R. Knox from Hills and Penn

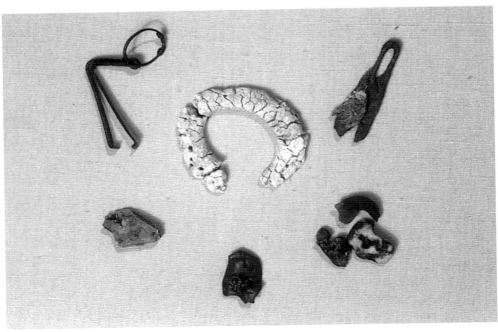

29 *Group of objects from cremations including a comb fragment, fused beads and a piece of a partially melted brooch.* Photograph by A. Kemp

things were placed on the pyre which was the same from one cemetery to another. Exactly where objects were located on the pyre may have had special meanings which are now lost to us.

Artefacts from cremations appear in sets. For example, brooches and beads are likely to occur together. This is similar to a female inhumation burial. Tweezers, shears and razors also tend to be found together. At Millgate, one set was found on its own ring. At both Spong Hill and Millgate, these toilet implements were miniature and some had blunted edges so they were never used for a practical purpose. They may have been made especially for burial. Toilet sets may represent men. Razors, tweezers and shears could all be used for cutting, shaving and plucking hair, a beard or a moustache. Some brooches show men's faces with impressive handle bar moustaches and this could be a representation of a male fashion for facial hair. In some instances, grave goods that were not functional, such as blunt blades and broken items, were included in the urn. These may be 'dead' or ritually 'killed' items with a symbolic meaning.

At first sight cremation has no obvious counterpart to the inhumation burials of men with sets of weapons. However, closer investigation does show that weapon fragments were sometimes placed in cremation urns. At Spong Hill, a cocked hat pommel from a sword was found in one urn and arrowheads were found in three others (Hills, C. 1977). Spearheads and shield bosses, which technically could have been put into an urn, are relatively large. These objects may have been on the funeral pyre and perhaps that was enough.

The objects found with both cremation and inhumation burials relate to the costume, warfare and daily work of the people and, therefore, have a significance much more far-reaching than mortuary practice. Ironically, the customs they followed in death allow us to learn a great deal about how the earliest Anglo-Saxons lived.

Different beliefs?

Most cemeteries contain both cremations and inhumations, although one rite usually significantly out-numbers the other. Both were in use at the same time and both extended over a long period. Why were different choices made about what to do with the dead?

At first glance, cremation may appear easy. All that is required is a bonfire and a small hole. However, as described above the truth is quite the opposite. In normal circumstances, human bodies do not burn easily. Cremations needed a lot of wood. Cutting down trees, chopping logs, moving them to the pyre site and building the pyre would all require time and effort. It must also be remembered that timber was an important resource, vital for heating and cooking, as well as a material for buildings, fences and tools. In cremation, the living are expending a great deal of time and effort on the dead. Inhumation, even if this meant digging a chamber rather than a simple grave, would take less time and use fewer resources.

Cremation is very visible. The burning pyre would be seen from a considerable distance. The pyre may have been located on higher ground or lit at night to ensure that the fire was observable, making some statement to the living. However, as pyre sites are not often found and we do not know the time of day the fires were started, these are only theories. Cremation also takes place over an extended period of time. All the preparations mentioned above need to be made, the body is burnt, the ashes are left to cool then they are gathered, placed in an urn and only then can they be interred in the ground.

Grave goods accompany both cremations and inhumations. Most of these are things the person would use or wear on a regular basis while alive. Food also accompanied both rites. The obvious conclusion is that these items were to be used again in the afterlife but we can never be sure. It has been noticed that there is no exact cremation equivalent to inhumation weapon burials. This could mean that cremation was not suitable for warriors. More prosaically, it may be that the Anglo-Saxons were practical people and could not fit a spearhead and shield boss into a pot with ease.

A striking difference between cremation and inhumation is what happens to the body. In cremation, the body is destroyed or perhaps transformed

(Williams, H. 1999) but bodies inhumed are initially left intact. This may represent a differing belief about what happened after death, such as how one actually journeyed to the afterlife.

Whatever the reason for choosing different burial rites, the two do not seem to be mutually exclusive within the same cemetery as they are found side-by-side. There may have been an acceptance of another's beliefs, or perhaps similar beliefs were expressed in different ways. Alternatively, society may have been less tolerant, but fistfights at the graveside have left no archaeological evidence.

Both cremation and inhumation were probably accompanied by rituals that have left no trace. For example, in present-day funerals, whether cremation or inhumation, mourners wear black and flowers are provided, particularly lilies often tied with purple ribbon. Whether we believe in an afterlife or not, we mourn the loss of loved ones and at the funeral we are allowed to weep openly and without embarrassment. The Anglo-Saxons whose remains we see were also people like us. Particular clothes may have been worn, jewellery may have been left off and certain words may have been spoken. Even if they believed in an afterlife where they would be re-united, they too may have mourned the loss of the people they loved.

3 In sickness and in health

If we want to know how advanced early Anglo-Saxon technology was, we can look at the jewellery, tools and weapons that were made in the period. To discover what plants they grew and what livestock they raised, we can examine the evidence of preserved seeds and animal bones from their farms, which in turn tells us what they ate. But what was it actually like to be an Anglo-Saxon person? To begin to appreciate life at this time, an idea of the physical well-being of the people is essential. In modern times, it is easy to become obsessed with health, some people choosing to spend hours at the gym preserving their physique and muscle tone while at the other end of the spectrum is the GP's friend who relishes giving minute descriptions of their latest ailments. But for the earliest English, staying healthy was not a hobby or a favourite topic of conversation, it was literally a matter of survival. So, how can we discover the state of health of people who lived 1,500 years ago? For a great deal of information we can turn to the people themselves.

Both inhumation and cremation burials contain human remains, usually in the form of bones and teeth. Information about illnesses suffered, toothache endured, accidents cursed and even violent encounters survived, are all locked away in this precious resource. Some details are difficult to extract and results can be controversial or frustratingly vague, but in the right circumstances it is even possible to ascertain the age and sex of an individual.

The study of human remains is known as palaeopathology but, as with everything in archaeology, there are limits. Soft parts of the body only survive in exceptional circumstances, usually when specially embalmed, in very dry or completely waterlogged conditions, and as yet no early Anglo-Saxon mummies or bog bodies have been recognised. If diseases, accidents and wounds did not leave traces on the bone there is little possibility of identifying their presence today. Lethal diseases and flesh wounds can be invisible to palaeopathologists. Visual and hearing impairment can also be impossible to detect.

There is, however, one source that can help put flesh back on the bones. A number of later Anglo-Saxon medical texts survive, and one of these is known as the *Lacnunga*. It is a complex document made up of many elements. It incorporates recipes for salves, washes, drinks and poultices with healing properties, alongside charms and prayers. The *Lacnunga* is drawn from a number of traditions including Greek and Roman and a significant proportion is Christian, at least on first appearance. However, although the surviving written version dates to AD 1000 some parts go back to pagan times (Pollington, S. 2000). Therefore, although there are dangers in using a source that was written down four centuries after the period under discussion, the clues it can provide are too valuable to disregard.

It can be seen that there are limitations to both palaeopathology and later historical sources but keeping this in mind it is still possible to build up a picture of the health of the early Anglo-Saxons, even if this picture is only an outline.

The survival of human remains

Careful examination of bones can give information about the age, sex and state of well-being of the individual to whom they belonged, but only if they survive. Spending 1500 years in the ground is not as safe as it might at first appear.

If people in the past chose to live in a location because of natural features, such as fertile land and dependable water supply, then these are likely to have appealed to communities who came after. Settlements can exist in the same place for hundreds of years and there is the chance that the new will obliterate the old. Sometimes a site may be abandoned but reused at a later time. The Anglo-Saxon cemetery at Wigston in Leicestershire was reused in relatively recent times as a modern cemetery! In the nineteenth century and more recently, the rail and road networks have destroyed or seriously damaged many archaeological sites. In some cases, objects were salvaged but human remains were not.

In arable areas, ploughing, often since the medieval era, has eroded away the upper layers of soil until today the machinery itself is cutting through the graves that lie beneath and is shattering bones in the process (**30**). At Empingham I in Rutland, only 14 graves were recovered, but the site had been so badly plough-damaged it is impossible to guess how many graves there were originally (Liddle, P., Glasswell, S. and Cooper, N. 2000). At Edix

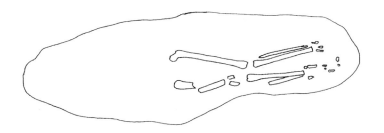

30 *Graves can suffer extensive damage from ploughing like this one from Empingham I.* Drawn by R. Knox

Hill, the bones were in good condition but numerous graves had been dug through in the 1840s when field drains were put in.

The soil itself often attacks bones. At the inhumation cemetery at Spong Hill, the acid soil had destroyed most of the bone from the 57 graves and at the royal cemetery at Sutton Hoo, some individuals survived as little more than a stain in the sand (Care Evans, A. 1986). At Alton and Norton, soil conditions had removed the surface of many bones making it extremely difficult to look for certain types of infection and injury. Of 63 graves from a cemetery at Portway, only three were well preserved and in one, all that was left of the occupant were three tooth crowns.

Cremations present another set of problems. In early excavations it was common practice to remove any recognisable artefacts, but to throw away the remaining ash and human remains. At cemeteries such as Spong Hill and Thurmaston, bones that have survived have been warped and shattered by fire. Also contributing to their incompleteness is the fact that not every single bone from the skeleton was collected and deposited in the urn in the first place. Teeth were often destroyed by the cremation process. In the past it was thought that little could be learnt from such remains but McKinley's work (1994) on the Spong Hill cremations shows this is far from the case.

The manner of excavation can also affect what information can be retrieved from human remains. Many Anglo-Saxon sites were 'excavated' in the nineteenth century or earlier. Some, such as Wigston in Leicestershire, are predominantly known from antiquarian drawings that often ignore the bones. In some older excavations, human remains were salvaged and either went into private collections, or into museums if one existed in the area. Many of these have subsequently been lost or all the bones from one site have been jumbled up. (Museum documentation may not seem exciting but it is important!) Even today, cemeteries can be discovered unexpectedly as at Lechlade. In this case, the site benefited from a modern and scientific excavation but had to be completed in just twelve weeks. Only the area directly under threat was examined which is thought to represent 50-75 per cent of the area of the cemetery.

Having survived all the mishaps and disasters that can befall human remains and reached the safety of the palaeopathologist's laboratory, what exactly is the story of the bones?

Breaking point

Anyone who has spent a few hours waiting in a casualty department will be able to picture images of people hobbling past with injured ankles or walking in, somewhat shakily, with a blood soaked tea towel wrapped around an injured hand. Many parents have been through the nerve-racking dash to the hospital with the child who has, for example, shoved a bead up her nose. Human beings are accident-prone creatures who can find danger in almost any environment. Judging from the evidence of their bones, our Anglo-Saxon predecessors were no different.

A fracture to a bone tends to leave a permanent visible mark. One of the most common to break was the collarbone or clavicle. At Alton, a woman who was over 45 when she died, had a very bent right collarbone, which was probably caused by a healed fracture. The 30- to 35-year-old man from grave 42 also had an old fracture to the clavicle, but in his case the bone had broken in two places. It was not properly aligned when it healed which resulted in a zigzag deformity exaggerating the curvature of the bone. At both Lechlade and Great Chesterford, three individuals broke a clavicle as did two more at Beckford. Calvin Wells suggested that broken collarbones were probably caused by falling onto the shoulder. In farming communities, falls must have been very common and breakages can be caused as easily as slipping in a muddy field (personal experience, S. Houghton). All the cases above had healed successfully.

Ribs were another fairly common injury site. A woman from West Stow had fractured a rib several years before she died, but it did not heal normally and became deformed. At Portway, a man had broken two ribs but these were well healed. A woman found in grave three had damaged three ribs, a large percentage of those which survived. It has been suggested that she may have suffered a crushing injury, where as many as 12 or even 20 ribs were involved. The vertebrae of the backbone can also be injured but this is much less common. At Great Chesterford, inhumation nine had a crushing fracture to the vertebrae probably caused by a fall.

Accidents involving the arms were a risk for the earliest English. The bones of the lower right arm, the radius and ulna, of a woman from Empingham I had been broken but mended successfully. Another woman from Great Chesterford did not fare so well. Although the fractured radius healed it was no longer straight. This affected the working of the joint and resulted in osteoarthritis developing at the elbow. Falling is again an explanation for such trauma but there are other possibilities. At Lechlade, the person in grave 86 had a greenstick fracture (the bone had not broken through completely) of the ulna, and at Beckford 2 the woman in grave 48 had a midshaft fracture of the ulna, both of which could have been sustained whilst holding up the arm to ward off a blow from an attacker.

The upper arm suffered injury less often but at Lechlade, the person in grave 106 had a left humerus 20mm shorter than the right due to the way the bone had healed. Not surprisingly, hands and fingers were the victims of accidents or clumsiness and this can also be seen in individuals at Lechlade.

Fractures to various bones in the leg appear to have been less common than in other parts of the body, but were still by no means rare. The woman from grave one at West Stow, with the broken ribs, had fractured the upper part of her lower leg (tibia). This was associated with bleeding and a dense growth of new bone. Although the leg healed it was not straightforward, and it has been suggested that the limb may not have been effectively splinted. Some people, such as at Edix Hill and Great Chesterford, were more fortunate and had well healed fractures to the leg bones. However, trauma involving the leg could be serious. At Norton, a young man from grave 91 had broken the bone in his right thigh (femur) which healed but was then 5cm shorter than the other because of muscles contracting violently when the accident, probably a severe fall or direct blow, occurred. It is likely that this was accompanied by significant blood loss and today victims of comparable injuries usually require a blood transfusion and surgery to repair the damage. The man from Norton required care for a lengthy period, as long as three months, and even when he recovered he would have walked with a limp, perhaps with restricted mobility. No grave goods were found with this man, which might suggest that he was of lower social standing or wealth. However, he still seems to have had access to a level of prolonged care that allowed him to recover from a life-threatening incident. Feet and toes also suffered as a result of stumbles, trips and falls and probably from being trodden on by livestock.

The head and face did not escape unscathed. Teeth were lost as a result of disease, but there is also evidence to suggest some were physically knocked out. From the cremated remains at Spong Hill, 12 cases were identified and one person from grave 288 at Morning Thorpe had three teeth removed in this manner. Six men from Lechlade had injuries to the head but the man from grave 65 had suffered a particularly nasty accident or vicious attack. He sustained multiple fractures to the right side of his skull, which would have distorted his face including his eye socket. There is evidence that healing had taken place, so he survived for at least a time and was over 45 when he died.

Not all injuries were accidental and some of the above may have been the result of violence. In other instances, evidence of anger or malice is much more clear. Sword wounds have been identified on individuals from the north to the south of England. At Edix Hill, three men had blows to the head that were probably inflicted with this weapon. The man from grave 48, who was between 25 and 35 at death, suffered what appears to be a glancing blow delivered from the front. A 45-year-old from grave 98 had a round depression in his skull suggesting a blade went clean through it, removing a roundel of bone. A long oval injury was inflicted on the person in grave 85 and its position suggests an opponent striking either from directly behind or directly in front. The first two men were both buried with spears and grave 48 contained a shield in addition. The third grave had been heavily disturbed and no grave goods were found. It seems likely that at least two of these men, buried with warriors' weapons, were wounded in battle but their injuries showed signs of healing proving they lived to tell the tale. If this is the case, it is interesting to compare the ages of the men. A man of 25 or even 35 is in the age range which might be expected for a warrior, but 45 was getting towards the older end of the scale by the standards of the time. Obviously retirement was not a luxury available to a warrior. Indeed, anyone who had lived that long might be particularly valued for their experience.

At Alton, one man had a straight cut 90mm long on the side of his skull that seemed to have come from a low angled blow from behind. A circular crater at the front of the head could also be from a glancing sword cut. Both of these wounds had healed. Was this man a warrior, or could this be evidence of a brigand's attack on a trader, or perhaps the wrath of a master vented on a slave? Any objects found with the man might help to narrow down the possibilities. However, archaeology is rarely so straightforward. In this case it is not known what, if any, grave goods were deposited with the man in grave 22 because only the head and chest area were uncovered. The rest of the grave extended into an unexcavated area in an adjoining garden.

A man from Lechlade had a cut to the left side of his head 83mm long caused by a narrow blade penetrating to a depth of up to 23mm. Part of the skull seems to have shattered as the blade was wrenched out sideways. Unlike the wounds described above, this showed no sign of healing, suggesting that it occurred at, or shortly before, death. At Norton, a middle-aged man had a jagged hole in his skull with a depression above it. A weapon is thought to be the cause, but no specific type is suggested. Spears were the most common type of weapon so this should be considered as a possibility for the puncture wound. Again, the man survived this violent encounter but when he did eventually die he was accompanied to his grave by a spear, a shield and a saex (a long, one edged knife).

Caution is always needed when attempting to interpret marks on bones that seem to have been caused by weapons. A 15-year-old from Alton had a clean cut across a kneecap. This was either caused by a sword shortly before death or possibly after death, by the archaeologist excavating the grave. Blades were not the only weapons used to cause injury. At both Norton and Great Chesterford, people had been struck on the head with blunt implements.

The above is a summary, not a complete list of wounds caused in anger. However, it is noticeable that the sample is mainly made up of men showing evidence of sword wounds to the head. Many were buried with weapons but, interestingly, none of this group was buried with swords. It can be suggested that most of these injuries happened in battle or armed combat. Most of the men survived, which suggests that if a warrior was alive at the end of a battle, even though hurt, his companions would attempt to get him home where he stood a chance of recovery. This may have been a luxury only available to the winning side. Those who died in combat seem under-represented and it may be that they were left exposed on the battlefield or were buried there in a communal grave. However, the writer is unaware of any such mass burials.

Although in many cases there is often evidence of physical recovery, this may not be the whole story. Brain damage may have occurred but there is no way of telling in which individuals, or how severely. It is unlikely that women had such a violence-free existence as it may appear. Many of the fractures and lost teeth described above as accidents could have been the result of blows. Often a fall is cited as the probable cause of an injury, but even a fall can be initiated by a push.

Bones can lose their density and become more prone to breaking due to osteoporosis. Today this is usually associated with older, postmenopausal ladies. Most Anglo-Saxon women did not live this long but one woman from Lechlade, who was over 45, showed signs of this condition.

The trauma described above is visible today because it can be seen on the bone, but this is only telling part of the story. A fall can tear a muscle, bruise flesh and bloody a nose just as easily as break a bone. Fractures themselves can be open, meaning the skin is broken and thus providing easy access into the body for infection. Any weapon slicing off part of the skull would first have to penetrate the scalp. Although the majority of damage to the soft tissue will leave no trace, in some instances the bone can preserve hints as to what might have occurred.

Today we are aware that dirt carries disease in the form of germs and bacteria. Most people who are bitten by a dog or who cut themselves while gardening will have an injection to protect against tetanus. This knowledge and technology is relatively modern. Even a small cut could lead to infection, but the Anglo-Saxons could not have known why. Some infections would be associated with injuries, but once inside the body could spread further via the blood. Evidence for this is sometimes preserved on the bone whose surface becomes rough and pitted due to the infection. At Lechlade, seven people display such evidence on the lower legs. Perhaps the shins were particularly prone to cuts and scrapes. However, one child, under two and a half years old, not only had affected leg bones, but also the interior of the skull suggesting a severe infection such as chronic meningitis. In view of the age, it must be considered that this was associated with the cause of death. At Empingham I, a man buried with two spears had chronic respiratory disease and would have been too ill to be an active warrior. At Edix Hill, 22 people had infections, but in most cases it was not possible to suggest a cause. One exception was a woman between 35 and 45 years of age. She had a crush fracture to one ankle, damage to the foot, and a thighbone twice the normal thickness. It seems likely that the ankle wound was open, allowing in the infection. She was buried with her left leg flexed at the hip and knee, perhaps because these joints could no longer be straightened.

Sometimes a new growth of bone will form where tendons or ligaments join the bone as a result of soft tissue damage or disease. High use or long-term stress on a group of muscles can also produce such growths. They can occur on many sites in the body including knees, fingers, arms, legs and spine. At Portway, bone growths suggest one woman twisted her ankle and another man pulled a muscle in his leg. These are not serious but could have been painful and restricted mobility until they healed. At Lechlade, one man appears to have injured his right hand, not a life-threatening incident, but inconvenient. Changes to the bones in the upper arms and legs of a young man from grave 121 suggest regular, strenuous exercise, possibly horse riding. Horses are usually associated with the upper ranks in society and are occasionally buried as grave goods. This man was buried with only a knife and a spear so, sadly, his horse must remain theoretical.

Dreaded diseases

Occasionally, some evidence for a potentially lethal disease is found, but this is only the tip of an iceberg with unknown proportions, and interpretation of the surviving signs can be difficult. For example, at Baston, Lincolnshire, one woman's left arm was shorter and slighter than the other. Multiple sclerosis has been suggested as a potential cause, but the diagnosis is not certain and it is not known how common MS was in Anglo-Saxon times. Polio, which is found in children and therefore can affect the growth of limbs, is perhaps a more likely explanation for the deformities of the woman from Baston (pers. comm. J. Wakely).

Although it is difficult to diagnose in archaeological remains, the presence of tuberculosis has been suggested on a number of Anglo-Saxon sites. People can catch both the human and bovine forms of TB. Before the Industrial Revolution (and the accompanying growth, squalor and overcrowding of the resulting cities) it is likely that bovine TB was the most common form in Britain. It could be contracted by drinking milk or eating meat from an infected animal. A cattle bone from an Anglo-Saxon pit near Spong Hill shows signs of TB suggesting that the local population were at least at risk. The cremations from Spong Hill included one older man who may have been a sufferer. Concretions in the lungs of a person from Sewerby may also be the result of TB as well as other cases from Alton, Lechlade, Edix Hill and Great Chesterford. The incubation period for TB can be a number of years. Taking into account the lifespan of many early Anglo-Saxons, it is possible that more people were infected but did not live long enough to develop any symptoms.

One disease, which today is particularly associated with medieval times, is leprosy. Many medieval dramas incorporate the sad image of the disfigured outcast, begging for a living. Leprosy, which is still a great problem today in certain areas of the world, attacks the nervous system leading to the loss of feeling. The skin, arterial blood vessels and tissue, particularly of the face, nose and eyes are also affected. The voice can become hoarse and eventually toes and fingers are lost. Small wonder that this infectious and disfiguring disease has caused such terror and revulsion over the centuries. Evidence for leprosy has been found in Anglo-Saxon skeletons, but it seems to have been very rare. Symptoms do not appear for two to seven years after infection so, as with TB, it is possible that people died before there was any evidence that they had contracted the disease. At Edix Hill, the woman in grave 18 had changes to her skull and both lower legs indicative of leprosy, although her hands and feet were not yet affected. It was probably not the cause of death despite being far enough advanced to have disfigured the face and caused significant discharge from the nose. This did not deter the people who buried her from going to considerable effort. She was buried on a bed in a deep grave with apsidal (curved) ends. Grave goods included a spindle whorl, a weaving batten, two knives, a key, a comb and a fossil sea urchin.

At Beckford, a man aged between 25 and 30 had extensive changes to his skeleton. Those toe bones that survived were severely deformed and all fingers were missing. He was buried with a spearhead, knife, scoop, bucket, strap end and possibly a buckle. Both of these individuals remained part of the community when they died and were not excluded from the local cemetery. Presumably they were not cast out of society during their illness either. Both of these burials suggest a medium to high status so perhaps these individuals were protected by wealth or position. However, the early Anglo-Saxons lived dispersed through the countryside so perhaps there was less pressure and necessity to make the very sick outcasts. It is only when people begin to live crowded together in towns and villages that infectious diseases can run rampant through communities. With no hospitals, the only care one could expect was from the family. Bonds of kinship seem to have been strong among the early Anglo-Saxons. Leaving emotional considerations aside, this was a practical essential. Only by working together, protecting and caring for each other, could these societies survive.

Aches and pains

Some medical conditions were very common in early Anglo-Saxon times. If preservation is sufficiently good, almost any Anglo-Saxon population studied will show signs of osteoarthritis. Until recently it was thought that this was a result of wear and tear on joints, but recent research has shown that it is a much more complex phenomenon with factors such as age, weight and genetics playing a part.

The spinal column is where osteoarthritis is most frequently visible in the earliest English, but many other areas of the body were affected including the hip, elbow, wrist, shoulder, fingers and toes. At Edix Hill, 85 per cent of adult skeletons suitable for study had spinal osteoarthritis, while 37 per cent of adults had it in other joints. In modern Britain, about 52 per cent of adults are affected. At Lechlade, almost everybody over 40 showed signs of the disease. The cremations at Spong Hill, despite the problems of working with fragmentary and burnt bone, suggested 16.6 per cent of the adult population had this condition and some individuals suffered with it in up to five joints.

Osteoarthritis can develop as a result of injury. At Empingham I, a woman's cervical vertebrae suggested an activity or occupation that exerted unequal stresses on her neck. However, an injury is another possible explanation, made all the more likely because she had two healed fractures on her right arm. A woman from Edix Hill seems to have suffered particularly badly in a number of ways. She was fairly short for an early Anglo-Saxon, 1.58m or about 5ft 2½in and of relatively slight build. (This begs the question of whether she was really of Romano-British origin, but there is not enough evidence to provide an answer.) An incident occurred in which she injured her knee, elbow and back with infection entering her body via the elbow wound. Osteoarthritis then developed in the elbow and knee with more changes visible in the thighbone, presumably due to having to alter the way she walked and moved. In addition, other damage was caused to her skeleton by very heavy work, which was too much for her build, involving the shoulder. She was buried with a new-born baby. It is impossible to say whether the baby was hers but death in childbirth has to be one explanation. She was found with a buckle at the chest, which may suggest that her belt was fastened above the 'bump' of a pregnant or newly-delivered woman. Beads were found under the chin and in the neck region but no brooches, suggesting that the usual tube dress was not being worn. It is very tempting to see this as evidence for the idea that she may have been of British origin. However, a tube dress can be sewn at the shoulders just as easily as fastening it with brooches.

A further condition affecting the spine is spondylolysis, a fracture of the vertebral arch. There may be no symptoms in life as perhaps was the case with three mild examples from Empingham I. However, it can become more serious resulting in increasing sciatic pain affecting the legs. It is difficult to know whether the people at Edix Hill and Great Chesterford with spondylolysis experienced this discomfort, but it is another possible source of hardship for the early Anglo-Saxons. The causes of the condition are significant. There is a genetic tendency to develop spondylolysis and it can be triggered by trauma, most often associated with manual labour and heavy lifting. Life was physically demanding and the traces of this are left on the bones.

Evidence for sinusitis has been found in a number of cemeteries and may also be connected with lifestyle. Sinusitis can cause a streaming nose, watering eyes, headache and pain in the face. The throat and upper respiratory tract can become infected. At Beckford, it is argued that irritation from hearths and fires was the cause, but one cremated individual from Spong Hill developed sinusitis as a result of a dental infection.

Teething Troubles

The preserved teeth and jaws of the earliest English have much to tell about the dental health of the period. Holes (caries) are found wherever there is a sample of teeth suitable for study, although often not in great numbers. In

1 *Artist's impression of the inhumation burial of the Glen Parva Lady, Leicestershire.* Painted by M. Codd, courtesy of Leicester City Museums Service

2 *The height of fashion in Anglo-Saxon glassware, these replica claw beakers show that the hollow claws not only looked stylish but also held extra liquor!* Photograph A. Kemp, courtesy of Jewry Wall Museum, Leicester

3 *Brooches come in many shapes and sizes. This is a selection of cruciform and small long-bow brooches from Empingham, Rutland.* Photograph by A. Kemp, courtesy of Rutland County Museum

4 *As iron objects corrode, the original form is preserved as seen here. However, once removed from the ground, such artefacts deteriorate quickly unless they are scientifically treated (conserved) or stored in very dry conditions.* Photograph by A. Kemp, courtesy of Jewry Wall Museum

5 *Florid cruciform brooches are found at the chest and probably fastened a cloak.* Photograph by A. Kemp, courtesy of Jewry Wall Museum, Leicester

6 *As the sixth century progressed, some brooches became more elaborate. Great square-headed brooches, like this one from Leicestershire, are found at the centre of the chest and probably fastened a cloak.* Photograph by A. Kemp, courtesy of Jewry Wall Museum, Leicester

7 *Female costumes show great variety in the number and types of brooches worn as well as in accompanying accessories.* Photograph courtesy of West Stow Anglo-Saxon Village Trust/St Edmundsbury Borough Council

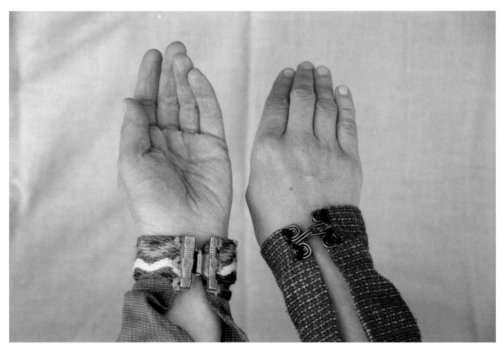

8 *These replica wrist clasps work like a hook and eye and show how the sleeves of women's under garments fastened.* Photograph by A. Kemp

9 *Many women wore an outer garment made from a tube of material, fastened at the shoulders with brooches. Beads were usually worn between the brooches rather than around the neck.* Photograph by R. Knox, courtesy of West Stow Anglo-Saxon Village Trust/St Edmundsbury Borough Council

10 *Crossing trails and dots are common patterns for beads and could, with skill, be applied to very small examples.* Photograph by A. Kemp, courtesy of Anglian Water

11 *Amber and glass beads are frequently found in female graves. This selection from Empingham, Rutland, shows just some of the designs and colours used.* Photograph by A. Kemp, courtesy of Rutland County Museum and Anglian Water

12 *Male costumes are reconstructed from numerous, disparate sources. Therefore, there is uncertainty over details such as length and embellishment of the tunic. Such factors may have been connected with wealth or status, reflecting the investment of time and materials.* Photograph by A. Kemp

13 *Some men may have used strips of cloth, similar to World War I puttees, as leg-bindings.* Photograph by A. Kemp, courtesy of Jewry Wall Museum, Leicester

14 *Little evidence survives for children's clothes. They may have worn miniature versions of the adult costume.*
Photograph by K. Glasswell

15 *Braid made on sets of square tablets could be used for decorative purposes but was strong enough for straps and belts.* Photograph by A. Kemp, courtesy of Jewry Wall Museum, Leicester

16 *Natural dyes available to the earliest English could produce a wide and beautiful range of colours.* Photograph by A. Kemp, courtesy of West Stow Anglo-Saxon Village Trust/ St Edmundsbury Borough Council

17 *Although a small community, keys found on the settlement at West Stow indicate that lockable doors were required.*
Photograph by A. Kemp, courtesy of West Stow Anglo–Saxon Village Trust/St Edmundsbury Borough Council

18 *Artist's impression of a very busy Anglo-Saxon settlement outside the crumbling walls of the former Roman town of Ratae Corieltauvorum (Leicester).* Painted by M. Codd, courtesy of City Museums Service, Leicester

19 *Early Anglo-Saxon houses leave little archaeological trace because materials such as brick and tile were not used in their construction.* Photograph by A. Kemp, courtesy of West Stow Anglo–Saxon Village Trust/St Edmundsbury Borough Council

20 *Sunken featured buildings probably fulfilled many purposes but using the pit as a floor surface was not practical in all soil types.* Photograph by A. Kemp, courtesy of West Stow Anglo–Saxon Village Trust/St Edmundsbury Borough Council

21 *Many methods for decorating pottery were employed. For some decorative schemes, potters used antler tines, carved with a huge variety of motifs, to impress into the damp clay.* Photograph A. Kemp courtesy of Jewry Wall Museum Leicester

22 *Although much early Anglo-Saxon pottery appears crude, some pieces like these of Illington-Lackford ware, would require great skill to make and decorate.* Photograph A. Kemp courtesy of Jewry Wall Museum, Leicester

23 *Precious metals were used for a number of objects, including jewellery like this exquisite square-headed brooch and wrist clasp from Empingham in Rutland.* Photograph by A. Kemp, courtesy of Rutland County Museum

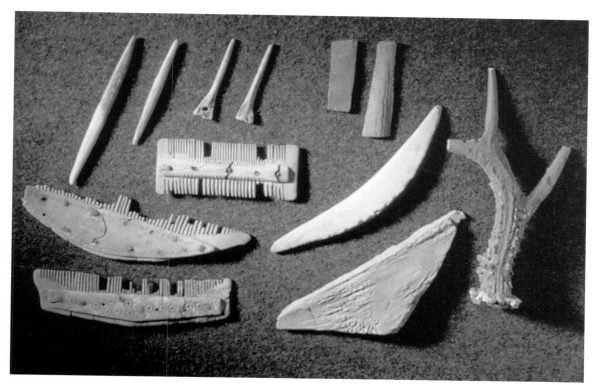

24 *Bone and antler were very versatile materials. Items at various stages of manufacture were found on the settlement at West Stow, showing that production took place on site.* Courtesy of West Stow Anglo-Saxon Village Trust/ St Edmundsbury Borough Council

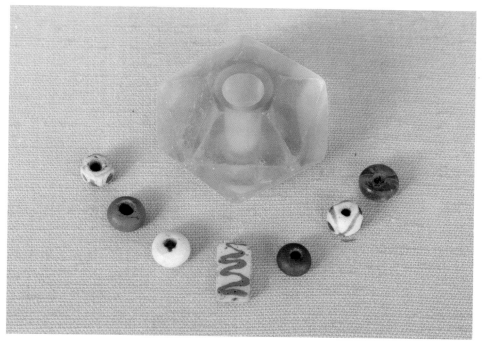

25 *Large, facetted rock crystals, like this example from Empingham in Rutland, were used as both beads and spindle whorls but may have been valued for amuletic properties.* Photograph by A. Kemp, courtesy of Rutland County Museum

26 *Artist's impression of a musician playing a horn, based on the eighth-century Canterbury Psalter.*
Drawn by S. Mallard

Anglo-Saxon times, too many sugary sweets and chocolate cannot be held responsible, so what was the cause? There are a number of factors resulting in caries, but studies have shown that a high percentage of carbohydrate in the diet can have an effect. They also increase in frequency with age because the individual has been exposed to infection for longer. At Empingham II, only three out of 45 juveniles had caries but this had risen to 23 out of 53 in the adult population. Some individuals, then as now, had more than one carious tooth.

Tooth wear in older people was a common and serious problem. Sometimes teeth became so worn down that the pulp inside was exposed. This could then lead to infection and the formation of an abscess as in the case of a person from Portway. Severe wear is thought to be caused by diet. Grain was ground into flour using a stone hand mill (quern). Tiny fragments of the quern would become detached, be incorporated in flour and hence the bread. Over the years, this abrasive diet took a heavy toll on the communities' teeth.

Abscesses can result from other infections and can be very painful. They can also result in the loss of a tooth. Like caries, abscesses are found in most places where Anglo-Saxon teeth are available for study. Other gum and dental diseases were experienced. There were also problems with deformed dentition. An impacted tooth was found in a person at Buckland. In the cremations at Spong Hill, another impacted tooth was erupting at 90 degrees from normal. At Alton, one 20-year-old man still had some of his milk teeth. There is also much evidence for tooth loss due to disease. At Alton, one man over 50 had lost so many teeth that he only had gum left to bite against.

Even today, many of us know how excruciating toothache is and although we may hate the dentist the option is there when we can bear the pain no longer. Some herbal painkillers available to the Anglo-Saxons may have given a little relief, but their suffering is beyond doubt. However, there are more serious implications. Tooth and gum disease can render the sufferer unable to eat which makes them weaker. Once an infection has taken hold, the body is more prone to others. Many individuals with bad dental health were old by Anglo-Saxon standards. What may seem to begin as a painful nuisance can thus develop into a potentially life threatening episode.

Signs of Hardship

Both bones and teeth can bear evidence of a time of deprivation, hardship and sickness. Pitting in the bones of the eye sockets can be caused by a lack of iron. This is known as cribra orbitalia. Most cemeteries contain a few individuals showing these changes. It is often attributed to poor diet. However, more recent research suggests that there may be enough iron in the food but it is not being absorbed. This is the body's self defence mechanism to fight infections, which need iron to thrive (Malim, T. and Hines, J. 1998). Bouts of chronic diarrhoea would have the same affect because food would pass through the body too quickly for iron and nutrients to be extracted. Therefore, it is still indicative of a time of crisis for the body, but not necessarily the same type as was originally thought. Estimates of people who were affected are again probably low because as a person recovered, the pitting could heal leaving no trace. As at Spong Hill, even when cribra orbitalia is present it is not necessarily serious.

Evidence for more significant periods of illness or times of deprivation during childhood can be preserved as lines on teeth, known as enamel hypoplasia. These bands of depressed lines or pits are caused by an episode of disease, particularly associated with fever, severe enough to stop the growth of teeth. Some people suffered on more than one occasion. At Empingham II, two people had two and three occurrences. The events took place between 2.8 and 4.5 years. Most people recovered and lived to adulthood, but one child had hypoplastic lines form at 2.8, 3.9 and 4.5 years and died between four and five. This has to suggest that this child was weakened too much to recover. The actual numbers of cases vary from cemetery to cemetery. At Norton in Cleveland, 50 per cent of people were affected but at Morning Thorpe only 10 per cent of people were affected. This does show that serious health problems were relatively common in childhood.

Flesh and blood

As discussed above, one of the few possible ways of understanding the full range of diseases affecting the soft tissue of the early Anglo-Saxons is a book called *Lacnunga,* written around AD 1000. Even if treatments changed between the two periods it is unlikely that ailments did.

The *Lacnunga* has many remedies relating to eye complaints, which suggests these were a common problem. Eye salves are suggested for dimness of the eye, eye-pain, tearful eyes and swellings. It is difficult to match these with the modern equivalent, but perhaps short-sightedness and conjunctivitis are possibilities. Ingredients used in cures for these maladies include penny-royal, feverfew, dill flowers, wormwood, cornflower and lily (**31**). Honey and deer's marrow were also used. One treatment requires a mixture that has been drained through a flax coloured cloth. The translation of the individual words is difficult so the exact meaning is uncertain. It could indicate a clean, undyed piece of fabric or perhaps a pale blue one. It has been suggested that if it is the latter then sympathetic magic is being invoked because the patient's eyes might well have been the same colour (Pollington, S. 2000). This raises the thorny issue of whether or not Anglo-Saxons had blond hair and blue eyes or whether they were a much more mixed group. It is not proposed that the argument is entered here, but perhaps DNA testing will give the answers in future years.

31 *Many of the plants found in a modern herb garden were used in Anglo-Saxon medicine.*
Photograph by A. Kemp

Losing the voice, insomnia, coughs, fainting and foot ache are some of the more minor complaints dealt with. For haemorrhoids, or piles (which must have been at least as painful then as they are now), a hot compress was recommended. More serious conditions listed are diarrhoea, heart pain, lung disease, asthma and possibly gout. As well as herb and plant elements, a range of other ingredients were utilised in remedies, such as the scrapings from a deerskin, swallow's nest, honey and warm dung from a calf.

The writings of the *Lacnunga* corroborate evidence from the surviving bones. A drink against knee pain and a cure for 'constant and malignant' joint pain are just two of those dealing with aches and discomfort, which may have been caused by osteoarthritis. The physical remains show that caries, abscesses and tooth wear were common and this is reflected by a cure against tooth pain which consists of a Christian prayer. Did it replace an earlier, pagan version? Indicators of small-scale accidents can be gleaned from the text such as what to do on losing a fingernail.

The *Lacnunga* can also give information about the treatment of early Anglo-Saxon patients. It exemplifies three aspects of Anglo-Saxon healing: herb and plant lore, surgery, spells and charms. The use of herbs and flowers has been illustrated above. However, a great many more than the ones mentioned here were employed in the salves, drinks, infusions and pottages used to combat a plethora of ills. In addition, steam was used in some cures. Inflammation could be treated with the steam from a mixture of pounded plants including ivy and cowslip, which were laid on a hot stone in a trough which then had a little water added to it. For bleeding haemorrhoids, steam is again incorporated into the cure with a hot quern stone (hand mill) providing the heat source.

Sometimes specific instructions are given for collecting plants used in the cures. Ironhard, in some instances, was to be gathered without using iron, such as a knife, to cut it. The hot compress for haemorrhoids required roots, which were not to be dug with iron, nor washed with water.

More invasive treatment was sometimes needed, but there is very little mention of surgery in the *Lacnunga*. One reference is for dealing with a burst eruption that is soaked in cold water until numb. Then four incisions are made around it, allowing it to drain. This is particularly interesting because of the use of cold water as an anaesthetic. Lowering body temperature had the additional advantage of slowing the flow of blood and thereby minimising its loss (pers. comm. A. Kemp). The afflictions the earliest English had to endure become all the more stomach churning when one remembers they did not have modern painkillers, although some plants such as henbane and poppy might have been used for their pain-killing qualities.

The text also gives an insight into what the Anglo-Saxons believed caused some of the illnesses they had to deal with. Today's medical understanding of infection and disease spread by bacteria and germs is relatively modern, originating in the nineteenth century. Early peoples found other explanations that made sense to them but may seem strange to us today. Those who might be responsible include the gods, witches and elves. There are also numerous charms against dwarves. It is not surprising that the supernatural was used to combat such works of evil. Many charms are preserved which on the surface seem to be Christian prayers and chants.

Others are clearly pagan in origin, including a group known as the 'Nine Herb Charm' or the 'Pagan Lay of the Nine Herbs'. In this the plants are sometimes spoken to directly by the writer and their powers are described. The full meanings are obscure. Another section speaks of the god Woden killing a serpent and cutting it into nine pieces from which come nine healing plants. The nine herbs include mugwort, described as the oldest of plants; waybread, mother of plants; cress; nettle, said to have fought against the serpent; atterlothe; maythe; and crab apple, the cure for the bite of another poison. A second charm that seems pagan in spirit is against a sudden stitch. It implies that the pain is caused by a little spear and aims to call this out of the afflicted person.

Even when cures incorporate Christian prayers they can contain rituals that seem more suitably pagan in origin. A woman who has not been able to bear a live child is told to go the grave of a dead man and step over it three times as she repeats specific phrases. She must then return to her husband and step over him three times while saying a different charm. Other rituals for women unable to keep a child alive, possibly because they could not breast feed, undertake other actions such as selling soil from the dead child's grave and spitting cow's milk into running water. These writings, therefore, give us a fascinating glimpse into attitudes towards the dead but because of the problems discussed above it is very difficult to know how far they can truly be read back to the earliest English, living four hundred years before. They also give a reminder that infant mortality may have been common, but was not necessarily any less tragic for the parents concerned.

Aspects of human comfort are also covered, such as how to get rid of lice. Cures are not given exclusively for humans. Some portions relate to pigs, sheep, cattle and horses.

When death came

Due to the way the skeleton grows, particularly the long bones and the pelvis, it is possible to estimate the age at which a person died. However, it is usually only feasible to suggest a range rather than a specific year of death. Adults between about 18 and 30 can be aged most accurately but it becomes more difficult with older people. There are additional complications because a person who is malnourished will develop more slowly than someone with an ample and nutritious diet. Tooth development and wear are another method of aging skeletons.

A further issue when attempting to assess life expectancy among the early English is the completeness of cemeteries. It is very uncommon for a burial ground to be excavated in its entirety. This means we are not looking at whole Anglo-Saxon populations but sections of them, which may not be representative.

In modern Britain, the death of a baby or young child is, thankfully, rare. It is such an unusual event that it is a tragedy we are mentally unprepared for. In England's past, infant mortality was more common and it has been estimated that between a third and a quarter of the population died before adulthood. This would imply that a large proportion of Anglo-Saxon remains recovered should be of babies and children, as at Norton where a third of people died before they were 18. However, burial evidence does not always conform to such ratios. At Empingham II, only two infants were found and at Buckland there were none. Can this be explained?

There are probably a combination of reasons for the under-representation of the very young. The site at Buckland was heavily disturbed. Infant bones are small, fragile and easily destroyed. At Great Chesterford, in contrast, 65 of 171 individuals were foetus and infant burials. Some of these were multiple burials, one containing six foetuses. At Westgarth Gardens, 19 infants and juveniles were discovered but 10 of these lay within nine square metres of each other. Therefore, in the two latter cases, burials of the very young were concentrated in certain areas and if these had been excluded from the excavation area, then a dramatically different picture would be presented. Very shallow infant burials were encountered at Great Chesterford and if this was common practice many such burials must have been destroyed by ploughing from the medieval period onwards. Human remains were discovered on the settlement site of West Stow and at least four of these were infants. So it can be argued that fewer infant and child remains are found because their bones are fragile, only require a shallow grave, may be clustered in unexcavated parts of the cemetery, or may have been interred within the bounds of the settlement.

Babies, without the aid of modern medicine, are stillborn or die for many reasons, but Lechlade sees a peak around the age of one year to 18 months. It is suggested that this could be associated with weaning, but alternatively, this is also the age at which babies begin to walk and climb. Toddlers like to explore and sadly this probably resulted in numerous deaths by misadventure.

When looking at the age of death among adults, it is very noticeable that men live longer than women. At Illington in Suffolk, the average age at death was 33.7 years for men and 27.6 years for women. Women's deaths peaked at Great Chesterford between 35 and 45 years, with a higher percentage of men living beyond 45. However, at Buckland the peak is between 20 and 30 years and at Beckford it is between 25 and 30.

It seems obvious that this is associated with childbirth, but is there any evidence for this? Occasionally the conclusion is inescapable, such as in a poignant case at Great Chesterford where the skeleton of a woman was discovered with a foetal skull in her pelvis. Woman die during pregnancy and childbirth for many reasons. Diabetes can develop which causes the baby to grow large and physically delivering it can then become very difficult or impossible. In other cases, a haemorrhage can occur while giving birth and without a blood transfusion a woman can simply bleed to death. Puerperal fever is an infection which enters the mother's body where the placenta was attached and this was very common until the 1930s, so is likely to have been widespread in early Anglo-Saxon times (pers. comm. J. Wakely). Both mother and baby are at risk of infection if the waters break but labour does not follow swiftly. Breech births, where the baby comes out bottom rather than head first, can result in fatalities. In some circumstances both mother and child can be lost.

Given all of the above it is not surprising that women could not expect to live as long as men. This is true natural childbirth. It is not known when early Anglo-Saxon women married and began to have children, but late teens or early twenties seems a reasonable guess. Today a woman's first pregnancy and birth tend to be regarded as the most difficult and giving birth to other children should be like 'shelling peas'. However, if Anglo-Saxon women are dying because of childbirth it must often have been with a subsequent child.

This perhaps highlights the very physically draining and damaging nature of multiple births in a society where life was already demanding.

There are always exceptions to the rule. At Empingham II, life expectancy appears to be lower than at other sites and the average age of death for men was earlier than women, 28 as opposed to 29 years. It is difficult to accurately calculate the age of older and old people and it is often only possible to say an individual was over a certain age. Most, but not all, cemeteries contain people over 45 years but Westgarth Gardens had some over 50. At Norton and Lechlade, a relatively large number of the population lived to be over 40, about five to six percent.

It must be emphasised that the ages given above are approximate and should be treated as orders of magnitude rather than exact chronological years. Age is judged by growth of teeth and long bones but the standard stages of these have been compiled by looking at modern populations, so there is the possibility that they were different in the past. Between 1984 and 1986, excavations at Christ Church, Spitalfields in London provided an excellent opportunity to test the accuracy of aging skeletons. The site was an eighteenth and nineteenth century crypt and many of the names, occupations and ages of death of the people excavated were known. Study of these skeletons showed that younger people tended to have their ages overestimated but older people's ages were underestimated.

A general pattern of Anglo-Saxon life expectancy can be suggested. Men were likely to live longer than women. Roughly a third of the population died before adulthood, around 18 years. Only about five percent survived to be over 40 and in some places this figure was a lot lower. Most of us today would expect to celebrate at least our 70th birthday so an Anglo-Saxon lifespan seems very short. However, things got far worse before they got better. During the Industrial Revolution, among the working classes in some cities, the average age at death dropped to as low as 17 years.

State of health

What, then, can be concluded about the health of the early Anglo-Saxons?

From the number of broken bones, it would seem that they were as accident prone as we are today, although a hard lifestyle or organised violence was probably more often the cause than unskilled DIY. The majority of breaks healed fairly well, which suggests an understanding of the techniques of splinting.

Infections have left traces of times of illness but these were again often survived. Serious diseases such as TB and leprosy were encountered, but not on the epidemic scale that would come with life in overcrowded, squalid towns.

The discomfort of common maladies and conditions such as haemorrhoids and headaches are evidenced by the numerous suggested treatments of the *Lacnunga*. This is supported by common finds of arthritic bones. Niggling caries and chronic dental abscesses were part of everyday life, especially for the older people.

Accidents and illnesses left many people with impaired hearing, sight and mobility. However, a blind lady can still spin and a deaf man can plough a field. Today we are trying to create a society that includes rather than discriminates against people with disabilities. Although it cannot be proved, it is possible that disability was so common in Anglo-Saxon times that people took their place in society and made whatever contribution they were able, regardless of physical or mental restrictions.

Taken together, the evidence forms a picture of a strong, physically active people who had enough medical knowledge to deal with a wide range of ills. This expertise was probably fairly widespread as there were no hospitals and it would be from family and neighbours that treatment and care came. Unlike later periods, this does mean that healthcare was not exclusively for those wealthy or important enough to be able to pay for it.

Women were particularly vulnerable during childbearing and many children did not live long enough to become adults. As people became older their health began to deteriorate rapidly, particularly their teeth and joints. By today's standards old age came early to the Anglo-Saxons.

4 What people looked like

The body beautiful?

If we want to know what Henry VIII looked like, we could simply examine the many portraits of him from life. Even allowing for some artistic flattery, we would be able to observe the sumptuous garments, his manly gait and his piggy eyes. Many paintings of his wives and courtiers are also available for study, so we could look at Henry within a context. Not only do these art works portray the appearance of Tudor nobility but because they are closely dated they also demonstrate changes in costume, hairstyle, jewellery and even make-up over an established period of time. Finding out about the appearance of poorer Tudor people would be more difficult, as artists painted people who could pay and were not so committed to recording their era for the benefit of later times. However, the lower classes are still seen often enough in the background of paintings and woodcuts for a general impression of their appearance to be built up. If we want to know what Hengist and Horsa (the traditional leaders of the first Anglo-Saxon settlements) looked like, we have nothing to go on at all. If the earliest English did make likenesses of their leaders, none have survived in a recognisable form. Were they the tall, athletic, blond bombshells of Germanic heroic legend or the wizened, wiry-haired, toothless peasants of television drama? Sources are available which allow a basic picture to be constructed. The objects left behind again have much to tell, as do the physical remains of the people themselves.

When the long bones of the arms and legs survive in a grave it is possible to estimate how tall the person was when they died. This may not be completely accurate because the technique was developed in the twentieth century to help identify modern people killed in mass disasters whose bodies were no longer visibly recognisable. Cemeteries up and down the country show that women commonly grew to around 168 to 170cm (around 5 ft 7in to 5ft 8in) and most burial grounds have men of 180cm and above (about 6ft). Many individuals were smaller, shorter women being around 150cm (5ft) and men 160cm (5ft 4in). However, the lower end of the scale probably includes young adults who may not have finished growing before they died. Height is dependant on genetic potential but requires sufficient nourishment and good health for the potential to be realised. The stature of the early Anglo-Saxons suggests that they were predisposed to be tall and many had a sufficiently varied diet to fulfil their natural propensity. In general, it is thought that the earliest English were taller than either the Romano-British who preceded them or the medieval population that followed.

Human bones indicate that the people were very muscular. Where a muscle attached to a bone this created a rough, lumpy area. The bigger the lump, the larger the muscle. Anglo-Saxon life was hard and physical. Farming, chopping wood and carrying water were just some of the everyday tasks that would have given them a physique that most people today can only achieve by relentless, sweaty hours in the gym.

One of the most exciting scientific techniques available today is the reconstruction of a person's appearance directly from their skull, bringing us literally face to face with our antecedents. This can be accomplished using sophisticated computer software or by physically building up from a cast of the skull. The latter method is not new. The first known scientific attempt was carried out by an anatomist called His in 1895 who was trying to ascertain whether an exhumed body was that of the composer Johann Sebastian Bach. His method was based on the thickness of soft tissue at particular points on the head using measurements taken from corpses as a guideline.

Reconstructions of archaeological skulls were made by scientists and sculptors from across the world following these principles. However, it came to light that two different groups of people working from the same skull could produce widely dissimilar results and the value of the process was called into question. Professor Mikhail Gerasimov began to work on the problem in the 1920s and placed great importance on the muscle structure rather than just the soft tissue. In Britain, Manchester University use both average soft tissue thickness and muscle data for their reconstructions. The process itself is a complex one. Archaeological skulls are often fragile and broken so conservation needs to be carried out in many cases before work can begin. Very fragile specimens are provided with internal support. A cast of plaster or cold-curing plastic is then made, a delicate operation in itself because nothing can be done which might damage the remains. All the holes on the skull, including the eye sockets must first be filled to prevent the casting material seeping into unwanted places but no features must be obscured in the process. The cast is measured and compared to the original to ensure that it is accurate.

For the best results, the age, sex, ethnic group and build of the individual should ideally be available and some of this, such as age and sex, may be discernible by examining the rest of the skeleton. These factors determine which set of soft tissue measurements are used. For example, anyone who has battled with weight problems will know that their face can look very different at times when they are overweight compared to when they are thinner. Either 21 or 34 anatomical points are marked on the cast where holes are drilled. Small wooden dowels are inserted which match the thickness of the soft tissue at each point. The inner and outer corners of the eyes are also marked and pegs are fitted to provide a framework for the nose. The main muscles are added and the muscle insertions on the bone give an idea of how strong these were. Layers of clay are used to build the face up to the top of the pegs. A final layer is applied to represent the skin and eyebrows, and eyelids are added. If the age of the person is known, wrinkles and creases can be added or even a typical hairstyle and make-up.

Not all features are straightforward. The nose is somewhat problematic because the main part contains no bones and so there is nothing to build on directly. However, features of the nasal cavity allow an approximation of the shape and size to be made. The dimensions of the mouth can be deduced but not the actual shape of the lips. In addition, little information is available for the ears but these are not usually crucial for recognising someone (Prag, J. and Neave, R. 1997).

Anglo-Saxon people have been the subject of facial reconstruction. One of these was a young woman from Glen Parva in Leicestershire who died around AD 500. The burial was discovered in the 1880s and at first it was thought she was a murder victim. A century later her skeleton was examined by Dr Jennifer Wakely who discovered she was about 5 ft 6in tall, well built and had died around the age of 22. There was no evidence for a cause of death. The objects found in her grave suggested she was fairly wealthy, being accompanied by a faceted crystal spindle whorl and a glass drinking vessel. Brooches, beads and an ivory bag ring indicated she was buried fully clothed, carrying what were probably prized possessions. In 2000, another piece of this ancient jigsaw was put back into place and it was finally possible to see the person behind the bones and objects. For those of us who have known her for many years, this was an emotional experience (**32**).

Winning smile?

Examining teeth from Anglo-Saxon burials proves that they suffered from tooth cavities and abscesses just as people do today. However, additional information suggests that there probably was no such thing as an Anglo-Saxon toothbrush. When a person eats, saliva and food debris build up on the teeth and form plaque, which is removed by brushing. If it is left, the plaque becomes a hard, mineralised deposit known as dental calculus. This is commonly seen among Anglo-Saxon communities. It varies greatly in degree with many adults having slight cases but some examples can be severe. In itself it is not harmful but to modern eyes at least, it is very unsightly. However, there is a possibility that calculus may give an indication of the general state of a person's health.

Chewing and a fibrous diet help to prevent the build up of plaque so if a person was unable to chew or had a restricted, soft diet this would predispose them to significant deposits of plaque. At Norton, the heaviest deposits seemed to be associated with individuals not able to chew properly due to tooth and gum disease. Breathing through the mouth may also speed up the

32 *Facial reconstruction of a woman buried at Glen Parva in Leicestershire around AD 500.*
Photograph by A. Kemp, courtesy of Jewry Wall Museum

development of plaque as food debris is dried onto the teeth. Therefore, the teeth of a person who had respiratory disease might be more likely to show severe calculus deposits. Nevertheless, even healthy people would develop this without a certain standard of oral hygiene. From a modern perspective, Anglo-Saxon smiles probably looked better if the lips were tightly shut.

Make-up and hairstyles

Roman written sources give a substantial amount of detail about the use of make-up throughout that era. Foundation, rouge, mascara and perfume were just some of the weapons in a Roman woman's arsenal of attraction. Cosmetic mortars, scoops and perfume bottles are recurrent finds on archaeological sites and back up the historical texts. Although the evidence is much more limited, it seems that Anglo-Saxon women also liked to enhance their appearance. Small copper alloy cones are interpreted as brushes for applying cosmetics such as eye shadow or blusher, the hairs or bristles having long since rotted away (**33**). Small scoops are found occasionally, often on a ring, which would have allowed them to be hung from a belt. They may have been used for removing small quantities of make-up, or its ingredients, from containers. Roman face packs and skin preparations were made from items including eggs, barley, honey and oyster shells. Foundation used sweat and dirt from sheep's wool, rouge came from ochre or the dregs of red wine and face powders included white lead. Mascara was produced from such interesting substances as bear's fat and squashed flies. Many other Roman cosmetics or components were exotic imports from across the Empire and would not have been available to the earliest English (Allason-Jones, L. 1989). However, the supply of dead flies and soot should have caused no problems, but these may

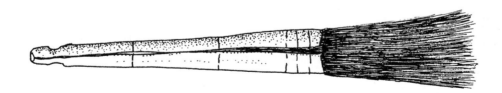

33 *Reconstruction drawing of a cosmetic brush (metal handle 8cm long)*. Drawn by R. Knox

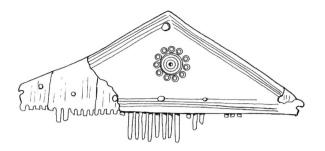

34 *The frequent occurrence of combs suggests that grooming was important to the earliest English (11cm long).* Drawn by R. Knox

35 *Razors found with cremations suggest that at least some men shaved (9cm long).* Redrawn by R. Knox from Hills and Penn

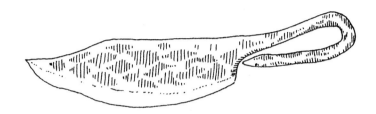

have been more suited to the darker, Mediterranean complexions. Ladies of Germanic and Scandinavian ancestry were probably paler skinned and lighter eyed and so may have utilised a different range of raw materials for their beauty products.

Long pins are found on the same ring as scoops but their exact use is uncertain. They would, however, have worked well for cleaning underneath the nails. Most of these toilet sets are found with adult women but one at Alton, Hampshire was buried with a child of about ten.

The lack of pictorial evidence means that little is known about early Anglo-Saxon hairstyles. Combs, made of bone and antler, are found with both women and men, suggesting that grooming was important to both genders (**34**). Wooden examples may have been used, as they were in earlier and later times, but they have not survived. It is assumed that women wore their hair long but practicality suggests it would be tied back, at least when working. Simple pony tails or elaborate styles incorporating plaits would require no more than a thong or braid to tie them and so would leave no archaeological trace. In contrast to the Roman period, hairpins seem to have been used only rarely.

Men's hairstyles are similarly obscure, but there are clues to the care men took particularly over their facial hair. Razors are common finds in cremations although rare in inhumations (**35**). This implies that at least a proportion of men shaved. However, men's faces are used as a decorative motif on certain types of brooch, usually with large or curly moustaches (**36**). Shears are another frequent find which could have been used for trimming hair, moustaches, and nails as well as, for example, cutting twine or yarn. Tweezers occur with men as well as women and could have been used for plucking eyebrows and so forth, but must have been useful for removing thorns and splinters besides. However, creating a particular look may have more significance than mere vanity. At the end of the first century AD, the Roman writer Tacitus produced a work describing many aspects of the way of life of the Germans. This contains a number of fascinating references to hairstyles. He records that among a tribe called the Suebi,

> It is a special characteristic of this nation to comb the hair sideways and tie it into a knot.
>
> (*The Germania*)

The Suebian knot is also represented on Roman sculpture and has been found on a surviving piece of hair. Dressing the hair to make a warrior look taller and more terrifying before going into battle was another tactic. The men of the Chatti, a more central Germanic people, left their beards and hair uncut when they reached manhood until they had killed an enemy. Tacitus was writing hundreds of years before the Anglo-Saxon period and he was discussing a vast area of diverse peoples, but the examples above serve to illustrate that symbols and rites of passage can be represented by details in appearance and this may have been true of the earliest English.

Miniature combs, tweezers, shears and razors are found repeatedly in cremation urns, suggesting that appearance had a particularly strong significance to individuals who were cremated. Why this should be is not clear. However, one theory concerns what happens when a body is burnt. The mourners watching a cremation see the corpse break down and be consumed by the fire, perhaps in itself releasing the soul. Even so a body might be needed in the afterlife, and toilet and grooming items might be required to help reconstruct the individual. Inhumation committed an unchanged body to the earth, although the early Anglo-Saxons must have been very aware that this too would decay.

Looking good, female costume

Many objects found in female graves relate to clothes or are dress accessories and these artefacts provide enough information to allow us to reconstruct the female costume (**colour plate 7**). However, although there are broad similarities across much of Anglo-Saxon England, there are also variations in detail depending on the region in which the woman was buried.

36 *Men's faces with moustaches often appear on brooches, like this one from Empingham.* Photograph by A. Kemp, courtesy of Anglian Water

Clothing fulfils a number of functions. In early Anglo-Saxon times, adult women probably spent significant periods of their lives either pregnant or breast-feeding. Anything they wore would need to be adaptable to these times. As well as protecting the wearer from the elements, clothing can be used as a method of displaying wealth and status.

Metal clasps are often found at the wrists of women buried in the Midlands, East Anglia and the North East, areas that Bede says were settled by the Angles (**37**). They are not found in the earliest graves of the settlements, but appear around AD 500. Wrist clasps were a hook and eye fastening occurring in many forms which changed and developed over time. They were usually decorated which suggests they were meant to be seen. They were worn on a long-sleeved dress, either fastening a slit in close fitting sleeves, or, if the sleeves were loose, allowing tight cuffs to be undone and rolled up. Wrist clasps could be sewn directly onto the fabric of the dress, but there is extensive evidence that they were also incorporated into decorative cuffs made of tablet woven braid (**colour plate 8**). In the southern, Saxon areas, it is presumed that women wore long sleeves which needed no fastenings or which used only organic materials such as cloth ties. It is not known whether those who could afford more than one set of clothes wore short sleeves in the summer. The dress may have had an opening down the front to allow for breast-feeding. This could have been tied using thin braid tapes. It has also been suggested this opening was fastened with a brooch (see below).

Brooches are one of the most common finds in female graves and suggest that a second garment was worn over the sleeved dress. Two brooches, one on each shoulder, are found most frequently (**colour plate 9**). These are interpreted as the fastenings for a dress, made simply from a tube of material.

The tube needed to be quite wide so there was enough cloth to pull up onto the shoulders without strangling the wearer. However, this also meant that the same tube dress could be worn throughout pregnancy because there was ample cloth to expand into. Removing one brooch would also allow the woman to breast feed easily.

All Anglo-Saxon garments were hand-spun and hand-woven, each item, therefore, representing a significant investment of time. Cutting elaborate patterns out of the cloth was extravagant and wasteful. Employing a design that used an uncut fabric was a practical use of a precious resource. Gowns had been made in this manner for hundreds of years over large geographical areas. Greek women, Iron Age Britons and first century Roman matronas would all have recognised the style. Brooches are sometimes found in matching pairs at the shoulders but unmatched pairs are also common. These can either be two brooches of the same general type or completely dissimilar brooches.

Sometimes a third brooch is found approximately in the middle of the chest. This may be a cloak fastening or a display of wealth. It may even be for both, when the woman came inside and took off her cloak she might then have pinned the brooch to her dress. In the Anglo-Saxon world, if you've got it, flaunt it. If the third brooch was fastened over the bead string it would have had the added bonus of holding the beads in place when the woman leant forward or bent over. Another possibility is that the third brooch fastened an

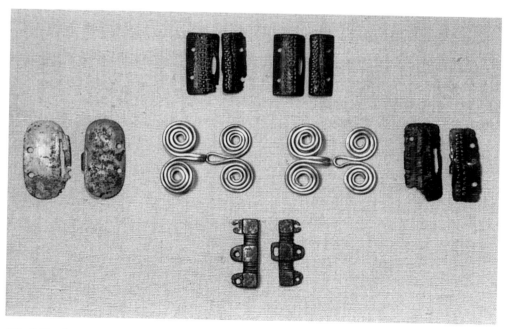

37 *Wrist clasps come in many types. This is just a selection from Empingham.* Photograph by A. Kemp, courtesy of Anglian Water

opening in the under-dress. However, these brooches were relatively bulky (**colour plates 5** & **6**). Also, bearing in mind these brooches were decorated, they would not be seen under the tube dress. If the brooch was worn so far up that it could be seen it would probably stick into the throat of the wearer and be uncomfortable. Sadly, human beings are not always rational and will wear decoration that cannot be seen and clothes that are uncomfortable, so this interpretation cannot be ruled out.

Large pins may have been used for the same purpose as the third brooch (**38**). They are regularly found in the chest and neck area. These pins come in a number of forms but are usually large, sturdy and decorated, and would be strong enough to hold a cloak in place. At Morning Thorpe, cloth was preserved in contact with such pins and it was usually of a coarse weave. In grave 140, textile was preserved with the shoulder brooches as well as the pin, and the two fabrics seemed to be different.

Rich graves can contain four brooches around the upper chest area. Two were probably used for a tube dress, but the purpose of the remaining pair is uncertain. However, in later periods, cloaks were fastened using two brooches with a braid, cord or a chain between them. In this arrangement, the brooches would sit over the collarbones, but the cloak would hang open, showing the

38 *Pins, like this one from Leicestershire, were used by women, possibly for fastening a cloak (11cm long).* Drawn by R. Knox

39 *Selection of some of the brooch types found in southern, 'Saxon' areas.* Drawn by R. Knox

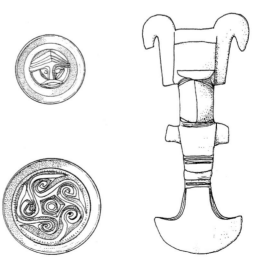

dress beneath. Frequently, women were buried wearing only one brooch, often in the centre of the chest. This would imply that it was being used for a cloak. The cloak itself may have been made from undyed wool to preserve its lanolin, which would act as natural waterproofing.

Many types of brooches occur. Some are a simple ring with a pin (annular brooches) and are found in most areas. Other round brooches are in the form of discs, saucers or small human faces (**39**). These occur more commonly in the south, in areas traditionally associated with the Saxons. Other clasps work on the principal of a safety pin. Cruciform, small-long, square-headed, florid cruciform and great square-headed all fall within this category of bow brooches (**40**). A number of types are widely distributed, but cruciform brooches are usually only found north of the Thames. Less commonly, brooches can be in the shape of birds. These tend to occur in Kent and the Isle of Wight, areas traditionally associated with Jutish settlers (**41**). Circular brooches, richly decorated with precious metals and garnets, occur in the same areas.

Even though brooches were functional, they were almost always decorated. Annular brooches often have incised lines, or ring and dot patterns made with a metal punch. Small-long brooches have moulded and punched decoration, but square-headed and cruciform brooches can be embellished with animals and human faces. White metal, often silver, and gold, are also used to coat the surface.

On a practical note, annular brooches are very difficult to put on because the cloth has to be forced through the central hole before the pin can be pushed through the fabric. Once in place, they are very secure and may have been left in place as the dress could still be removed and put on again. However, they would be far from ideal for a woman breastfeeding. Annular brooches also leave their pins exposed and are hazards for anyone looking after babies or young children. Bow brooches have the advantage of covering the pin and are also very easy to put on and take off.

A significant number of graves are found with no brooches. This might mean that the person was not buried in a tube dress, perhaps because they were poorer or a slave, but there are other possibilities. The long-sleeved dress which is usually thought of as an under garment may have been the most usual gown, with a tube dress only being worn for special occasions. Alternatively, the absence of metal fittings does not rule out the presence of a second garment. Tube dresses could easily have had a sewn or laced fastening. Late Roman clothes used no metal components. By the third century, Romano-British women were wearing long under-tunics with tight sleeves that reached to below the elbow. Over this came a gown known as a Gallic coat, which reached the mid-calf, had wide sleeves to the elbow and a slit, rounded, or V-shaped neck. Traditionally, it was not belted, garments using a belt or sash being associated with slaves. A long stole could be worn around the shoulders and evidence from France suggests that ankle- and knee-length

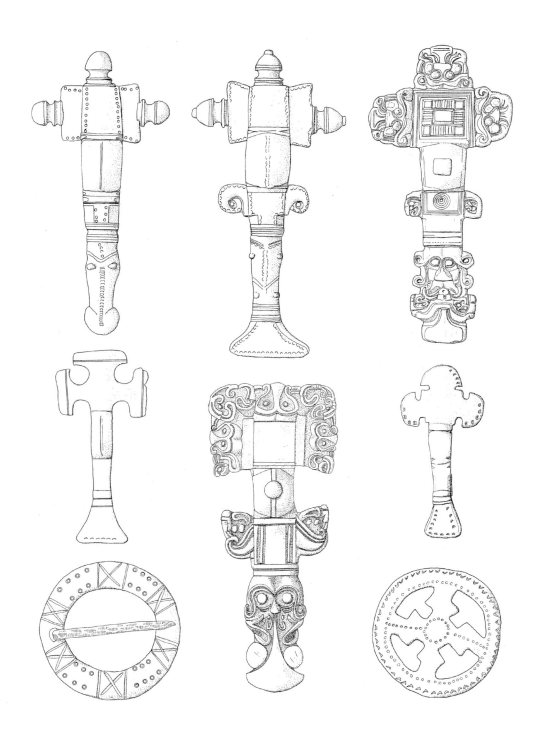

40 *Some of the brooch types common in areas which Bede associated with the Angles.*
Drawn by R. Knox

cloth socks were worn. Taken together, this is an elaborate clothing set and the sheer volume of fabric perhaps indicates its value. This illustrates that Anglo-Saxon graves found with no metal brooches cannot safely be assumed to be those of poor slaves with only basic clothes. It is possible that some of these women were descended from the Romano-British population and chose to keep their own traditional costume alive. Until there is more conclusive evidence, any or all of these interpretations are valid possibilities.

Swags or festoons of beads hung between the brooches (**colour plate 11**). From the point of view of wealth or prestige this arrangement has the advantage of displaying all your beads at once, none being hidden around the back of the neck. Beads were very decorative and many were made from glass of one or more colours. Combinations of blue, yellow, white, red, green and black were the most common, but brown, purple and turquoise were also used. Beads were decorated with patterns that included spots, wavy lines and crossing trails, with or without extra spots (**colour plate 10**). On occasions, a second colour added to a bead may not seem to form a design at all but rather a clumsy splodge. Experimentation has shown that this can often occur when the main body of the bead is too hot, so attempts to apply a second colour merely drag through the base glass rather than sitting on top of it. Gold foil encased in glass, rock crystal (which is clear and colourless) and bone were all used for beads.

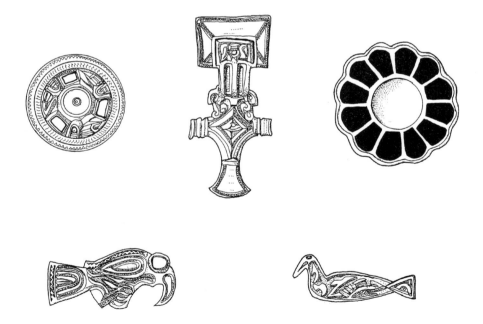

41 *Brooches from Kent and the Isle of Wight. Top right is a Frankish import. Bird brooches were also more common in what is now France.* Redrawn by R. Knox from Arnold and Evison

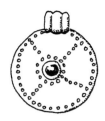

42 *Pendants were often incorporated into bead strings, like this one with an interlace design from Buckland and this scutiform example.* Redrawn by R. Knox from Evison

43 *By the seventh century, pendants often included stones such as garnets like these from Lechlade.* Redrawn by R. Knox from Boyle, Jennings and Miles

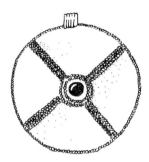

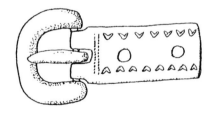

44 *Buckle from a woman's grave at Empingham.* Redrawn by R. Knox from Timby

Amber was worn in small quantities from early in the period but became much more popular. By the end of the sixth century it was the predominant bead material. Jet also occurs, but is rare. Long bead strings may only have been worn 'for best'. They get in the way of many occupations, are prone to getting caught and snapped, and can become positively dangerous when cooking over an open fire. They are also irresistible to babies. By the end of the sixth century costume was changing, the tube dress went out of fashion and with it, long bead festoons. Instead, necklaces were made from silver wire rings, beads and sometimes pendants, including ones made from amethyst.

Pendants occur in many forms and change through time. Circular scutiform (shield-shaped) pendants, often of silver, with a small raised boss in the centre, were incorporated into bead strings (**42**). Similar examples but with animal or human decorative motifs are known as bracteates. Towards the end of the early Anglo-Saxon period, more pendants with stones set in them appear (**43**).

Buckles from graves suggest that belts were worn around the waist (**44**). Numerous articles are found in positions that suggest they were originally hanging from a belt. Girdle hangers (see below), purses and knives all fall into this category. The purpose of some objects is unclear. Girdle hangers are found in East Anglia, the Midlands and the North East. They are shaped like an upside-down T, are made of copper alloy, and are usually, but not always found in pairs, either matching or odd (**45**). Although it has been suggested that these were symbolic keys and show that a woman was married, there is little evidence to support this. They are not common enough to have been buried with every married woman. A slightly different interpretation is that they show that the woman was the head female of her family. Girdle hangers can be found with girls as young as fifteen and although this does not rule out the previous theory it should not be accepted without question. No two pairs are exactly alike, with differences in shape and decoration, including the addition of birds' heads on the tines of examples from Morning Thorpe and Wigston, Leicester. Girdle hangers are most frequently, but not exclusively,

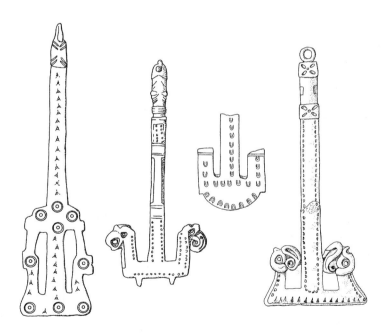

45 *Girdle hangers vary considerably in detail. Their precise function is unknown.* Drawn by R. Knox

found with annular brooches. In some cemeteries, a large pin is incorporated into this set. Further research may find more subtle symbolic meaning for these objects.

The early Anglo-Saxons did not wear wedding rings and finger rings are not often found in graves. Surviving examples fall into two main categories, those made of flat bands of metal and those of wire (**46**). Both are often in silver, but gold and copper alloy alternatives exist. The flat band rings can encircle the finger once but often spiral up for an extra half or full turn. Punched and incised decoration was often incorporated into the design. Wire rings usually have a spiralled bezel.

Bracelets are equally uncommon (**47**). At Broughton Lodge, they were found in two graves, still around the wrists of their owners. Both bracelets were similar but the one from grave nine was more complete. It was made of silver and wound up the arm for at least one and a half turns. This had the bonus of displaying twice as much of the front of the wrist as it did of the back. The front section was wider than the band at the rear and corrugated. Incised lines and punch motifs were used for decoration. The more frag-

46 *Finger rings are not common but come in two main types: one made of wire, the other of sheet metal.* Redrawn by R. Knox from Boyle, Jennings and Miles

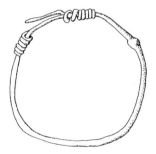

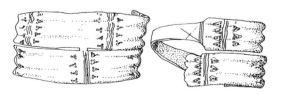

47 *Bracelets are rare. The wire example is from Buckland and the sheet metal one is from Broughton Lodge.* Redrawn by R. Knox from Evison and Sherlock and Welch

48 *Large rings of bone, antler and metal were used for suspending items from a waist belt, such as the latch lifters seen here.* Photograph by A. Kemp, courtesy of Jewry Wall Museum, Leicester.

mentary bracelet from grave three had plain, corrugated portions but the flat area had been adorned with a circular stamp motif. Two bracelets from the same grave at Norton again spiralled up the wrist and were made of silver. They were not corrugated, but were broader at the front increasing to an apex on both the upper and lower turn. Further embellishment was added with two punch designs, one circular and one triangular. A second type of bracelet was made of plain wire. Each end was wound around the main band, so that it could be enlarged to slip over the hand but would then contract so as not to fall off.

Larger rings of antler or copper alloy are frequently found at the waist and are thought to have been used to suspend other items from (**48**). Large, ivory rings are all that usually remain of the early English equivalent to a handbag. The ivory served as the mouth of the bag or purse. The bag itself was made probably of leather or fabric and does not often survive. This ivory would have been an expensive import and examples are usually found in wealthy burials. Logically, the pouch element of the purse would have been laced onto the ring so that the ivory could be displayed. However, excavations at West Heslerton have recovered two examples where substantial amounts of leather survive and it seems that the ivory was completely covered.

In some graves, items are found closely grouped together suggesting that they were originally held in a bag, which has left no trace. Presumably this means that pouches, bags or purses were also made just from cloth or leather

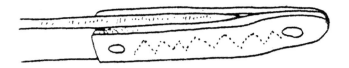

49 *Belts, and possibly garter ties, often terminated in a metal strap end.*
Drawn by R. Knox

that have rotted without trace. Medieval examples of similar objects can incorporate decorative motifs and tassels and it is possible that similar adornments were added to Anglo-Saxon examples.

Leg covers were probably worn. Graves often contain one strap end associated with a belt but occasionally a greater number are discovered (**49**). In these instances, strap ends may have come from garters, or ties used to fasten leg bindings or stockings. Shoes were made of leather, but do not survive in the grave so consequently, very little is known about them. However, they need not have been plain. Roman and medieval shoes were sometimes of dyed or open-work leather. It is not known what, if any, underwear was worn by Anglo-Saxon women.

Although incorporating some of the elements described above and existing alongside it, a distinct fashion appears concentrated on the Isle of Wight and Kent, areas traditionally associated with Jutish settlers. This style is more difficult to understand. Instead of a brooch at each shoulder, three brooches, or two brooches and a pin are found in a row between the neck and waist. This can be reconstructed as a wrap-over dress, which fastens down the front. A similar garment was found in the burial of a princess from Paris. However, the princess was not a Jute, but a Frank. It is thought that the Jutes had important links with the Franks from the early sixth century, which were consolidated in AD 560 when King Ethelbert of Kent married the Merovingian Princess Bertha. This special relationship is reflected in costume and perhaps Bertha was not the only high-born lady to cross the Channel as a bride. Material evidence of contact comes from cemeteries such as Buckland, with its significant proportion of imported Frankish objects.

The wrap-over dress may not have been belted and brooches are sometimes found near the hips from which other items seem to have been suspended. The position of the beads is also interesting because they regularly lie in a vertical line between the throat and waist. In some cases, it may be that as the body decayed, the beads fell into an odd position, but the vertical orientation occurs in enough graves to suggest it was deliberate. Beads may simply have been suspended in a vertical string but would be more secure if fastened to the dress at both the upper and lower ends. Alternatively, the beads may have been sewn onto the front edge of the wrap-over dress, perhaps even functioning like buttons.

The richest women in this community are occasionally found with gold brocaded braids, most of which date to the middle and later sixth century. The metal itself comprises of narrow, flat strips cut from gold foil and forms part of the original tablet weaving (described below), making geometric patterns such as crosses, steps and chevrons, although a more complex interlace motif is known from an example at Chessell Down. In most cases, the fabric threads have disappeared and only the gold survives, usually on or near the skull. The metallic adorned section of the band varies in length but is not usually sufficient to encircle the whole head. However, the gold could have been woven into only part of the braid, the front section where it would create maximum impact. The rest of the band may have been hidden by hair and fastened at the back of the head. Conversely the braid could have been long enough to tie and for the ends to hang loose as ribbons.

These brocaded bands are concentrated in Kent, but are more numerous on the continent. It is most likely that they are another manifestation of the strong Frankish influence on the area. Contemporary texts by Gregory of Tours and Venantius Fortunatus describe aristocratic and royal Frankish personages wearing clothes adorned with golden belts and cuffs. Gold-decorated headbands are described as being worn around the head directly onto the hair, but some women wore them on top of a veil. Surviving examples usually have gold round only part of the head, as in England, but in some cases would have been long enough to completely encircle it. In examples where the fabric element survives, it is usually silk. Silk is not found in early Anglo-Saxon England, which suggests that if the English bands incorporated this material they were probably not only copies of Frankish fashion, but were actually imported. In either case, these would have been very costly items and on the continent are found in aristocratic and royal graves. Do those from Kent also come from the burials of princesses?

From the above, it can be seen that where a woman lived affected what she wore. Is there a reason for this? Bede records that the settlers who came to Britain were Angles, Saxons and Jutes who made their homes in different parts of the country:

> From the Jutes are descended the people of Kent and the Isle of Wight and those in the province of the West Saxons opposite the Isle of Wight...From the Saxons...came the East, South and West Saxons. And from the Angles...are descended the East and Middle Angles, the Mercians, all the Northumbrian stock...
>
> (Bede, *Ecclesiastical History*)

This roughly corresponds to the regions seen in costume variation, the Angles with wrist clasps and girdle hangers, the Saxons with saucer brooches and the Jutes with their dressing gowns. But is it really as simple as this? Bede was writing two hundred years after the event, so is he correct? The settlements took place over a long period of time. It would be more reasonable to suppose that although one area might be heavily settled by Saxons, there might be immigrants of different races in the area and this seems to be supported by archaeology (**50**). Other peoples, who probably took part in the settlements, perhaps in smaller numbers, included the Frisians and Franks.

When the Anglo-Saxons came to Britain there were already Romano-British people living here. It might have been important to the settlers to show that they were different. When newcomers, arrived they may have preferred to look like the other immigrants rather than Britons, even if that meant changing the way they dressed. When the Anglo-Saxons had finished fighting the Britons, they often fought each other as numerous kingdoms grew up. What people wore might have been important in showing allegiance to a realm. Dressing to show loyalty or for identification is something we still do today. A Scot might wear a kilt on a special occasion even if he now lives in England. It is perhaps most clearly demonstrated by the shirts and scarves worn by football fans, which at the same time express an individual's loyalty and identify them with the group to which they belong.

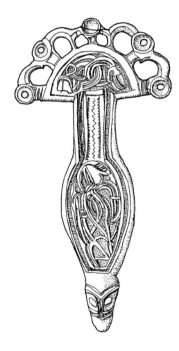

50 *Radiate head brooch of a type usually associated with the 'Franks' but found in 'Anglian' Rutland (8.3cm long).* Drawn by R. Knox

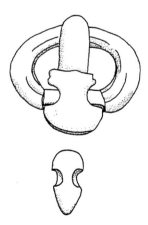

51 *This buckle is of 'Frankish' type. It is found in England with both men and women.* Drawn by R. Knox

Dressed to kill, male costume

Direct English evidence for male costume in the fifth and sixth centuries is scant. The only item found directly connected to men's clothes tends to be a buckle. Therefore, a number of other sources have to be used to try to build up a picture of what Anglo-Saxon men wore. These sources are continental Roman sculpture and historical texts, Scandinavian and German bog finds, and later Anglo-Saxon manuscripts.

Taking all these sources into consideration, the following can be suggested (**colour plate 12**). Men wore a tunic that came down to the knee or above. This was fastened at the waist with a belt. Belt buckles are found at the waist in graves and come in a number of different types (**51**). Most are relatively simple. Many have a plate that fastened onto the belt. Rectangular, square and the elongated triangular forms were popular. Belts were probably made of leather but tablet weaving is another possibility. Strap ends of copper alloy are also found in association with belts. Cloth preserved in contact with buckles suggests that tunics were made from wool and less commonly from linen. Not all men's graves contain a buckle, so some probably used purely organic belts, tied in a knot. Germanic tunics are represented with both long and short sleeves. A cremation urn from Spong Hill was accompanied by a lid in the form of a man (looking rather depressed) sitting in a chair. The details of his clothes are not distinct, but he appears to be wearing a long-sleeved tunic with cuffs. The Sutton Hoo helmet, an early seventh-century object, is decorated with figures of warriors wearing an alternative style of garment. Here, knee-length, wrap-over tunics with broad bands of decoration and wide belts are portrayed (**52**). A number of the figures are wearing headdresses and may be taking part in a ritual, so perhaps the costume shown was only worn for special purposes.

It is not certain whether or not male tunics were adorned with tablet weaving because there were no metal fastenings or accessories to preserve traces of braid. However, a tunic found in a peat bog at Thorsberg, Germany, was edged with tablet woven braid. The second richest Anglo-Saxon grave from England also suggests that men may have liked embellishments. The early seventh century burial from Taplow contained woollen tablet weaving brocaded with gold, like those found with rich Kentish women described above. Two pieces of gold braid were recovered with lozenge, rectangle and cross motifs being identifiable. Although the braids were of different thickness, they seem to have been a matching set. Unfortunately, the grave was excavated during the Victorian period and it was poorly recorded. It is not certain what the gold brocades decorated but it may have been a baldric for carrying a sword and belt.

Trousers may have been fairly baggy but held tight against the legs with bindings like First World War puttees (**colour plate 13**). Leg ties and bindings have again been discovered in peat bogs. These gave extra protection

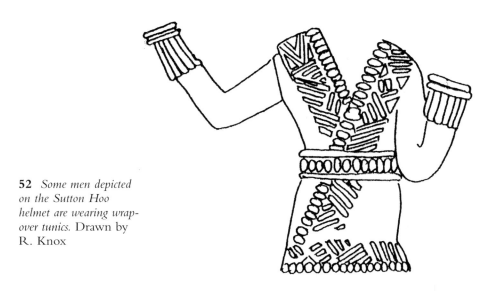

52 *Some men depicted on the Sutton Hoo helmet are wearing wrap-over tunics.* Drawn by R. Knox

to the shins, which may have been useful for the physical lifestyle led by Anglo-Saxon men. Puttees would also stop cloth catching and tearing on bushes, fences and so forth. Considering the time spent on fabric production it is not unreasonable to think that they took some measures to protect their clothes. Puttees are long, narrow strips of cloth and could have been specially woven. Looms of different widths were found at West Stow. However, they could have been made by cutting up and re-using old garments that were worn or ripped. Other Germanic trousers may have been tight, as represented on the Spong man. Roman sculptures seem to represent belted trousers but buckles are not obvious. If both the trousers and tunic were belted, then two buckles might commonly be found in the graves. However, when this is the case, one is often found away from the body, near the head or feet and is associated with a shield, probably coming from a carrying strap. Drawstring trousers would tie easily but one pair of trousers from Schlewig-Holstein had belt loops. It is unlikely that every pair of trousers would have been the same and both types may have co-existed.

Bog trousers have been found with an integral foot, but it is not known how common this was. Socks made of cloth could have been worn, but do not survive. Evidence for men's shoes is also lacking, suggesting they were made of leather, without the use of hobnails, which were commonly incorporated into Roman shoes. Leather shoes are comfortable and can be long lasting if not regularly used on stone surfaces, such as hard, Roman roads. The Spong man is shown bare foot. The Anglo-Saxon language has words for several types of shoe, including slippers and ones made of rawhide.

In cold or bad weather, cloaks, possibly with a hood, were probably worn. Roman sculpture represents Germanic prisoners in both short and knee length examples. Sixth-century Norwegian cloaks have been discovered with multicoloured tablet woven borders, enhanced with embroidery, suggesting that cloaks, although functional could be very ostentatious and prestigious garments. As well as cloth, fur was probably used for warm outdoor wear (Owen–Crocker, G. 1986). In addition to hoods, hats could have been worn. A round, flat-topped pillbox type hat is shown on the man from Spong Hill.

As discussed above, late Roman costume worn in Britain used no metal fastenings. Like women, men wore an under-tunic with a Gallic coat over the top, although men's garments were shorter. These would leave no archaeo-logical trace, but similar clothes could have been worn by some sections of the early English community.

Children's clothes

Fewer items are found in children's graves. It seems likely that they wore clothes similar to adults (**colour plate 14**). Many cemeteries contain a small number of children buried with the full range of brooches, beads and acces-sories which would be found with an adult. However, this may indicate more about social status than children's costume. More commonly, one or two beads would be found with a juvenile. Buckles occur regularly suggesting their garments could be belted. In some instances where no buckle occurs, a knife is found which implies that belts could be completely organic, perhaps made of tablet weaving and simply tied. It is not known if babies were swaddled or allowed to roll free.

5 Hearth and home

Most people spent their day-to-day lives producing what they needed to survive. This included tools, food, clothes, pottery, woodwork, and buildings. Men, women and children probably all had their own jobs to do, but it can be very difficult to say who did what. For example, equipment for spinning is found buried with women so this would seem to be one of their tasks but we can only guess at who was in charge of the vegetable patch. The role of children is also difficult to establish but it is likely that they learnt certain jobs from a very early age. There were no schools, as we understand them today, and it can be argued that childhood was spent learning the tasks an individual needed to survive as an adult. If a carefree, lazy childhood existed at all, it is likely to have been short.

Houses, workshops and stores

After the abundance of evidence for burial, information relating to how the Anglo-Saxons lived is sparse in contrast. Their buildings were made of timber, thatch and other materials that decompose completely (**colour plate 18**). This means that when trying to reconstruct what they looked like, the main source of evidence is what survives in the ground. In-filled holes left by rotted posts, trenches where plank walls once stood and enigmatic pits are all the archaeologist has to go on. In many cases, more than one interpretation of these features is possible. As these remains are often in the form of colour changes in the soil they are hard to identify. Victorian antiquarians could hardly miss a Roman villa with its stonewall foundations and clay roof tiles, but in these early days of archaeology an Anglo-Saxon building could be dug out before it was noticed.

There are some cases where there is evidence that Roman villa sites were reused, with indications of Anglo-Saxon occupation found within the complex. In recent years, buildings of Anglo-Saxon types have been discovered inside or close by Roman towns such as Leicester. However, as these areas have often continued to be occupied ever since, little has survived and it is difficult to construct a picture of what life entailed in these situations. Most of the earliest English lived in farmsteads spread out across the countryside with towns and villages not developing in earnest until middle Saxon times. The relatively small scale of the settlements contributes to their elusiveness. Therefore, the number of settlements found is considerably fewer than cemeteries, although modern excavation practices are redressing the balance.

One farm would require many buildings. The people needed somewhere to live, but workshops for a variety of activities were also necessary. In addition, farming equipment and tools had to be stored. Successfully providing food for the year called for storage that would protect the harvest surplus from infestation and decay. Hay, for feeding livestock over the winter, would survive better under cover and, on occasion, it may also have been necessary to bring livestock into barns and stables.

The same farmsteads could be used for generations. When a building came to the end of its practical life, a replacement was usually constructed nearby rather than directly on top. This had the advantage that the old one was still available while the new was being built. However, this practice resulted in the settlement gradually shifting its position. Excavations tend to uncover the plans for all of these buildings giving the impression of large settlements, but in fact only a selection stood at the same time.

Two main types of building are usually found and a variety of construction techniques were employed. Rectangular patterns of postholes are the remains

53 *Houses presumably had windows that closed with shutters at night or in bad weather.* Photograph by A. Kemp, courtesy of West Stow Village Trust/St Edmundsbury Borough Council

54 *Iron latch lifter and keys tend to be found with women rather than men (13cm long).* Drawn by R. Knox

of structures sometimes referred to as 'halls' (**colour plate 19**). These were probably dwellings in many cases, although at Mucking some may have been sheds or partially enclosed shelters. Only small quantities of wattle and daub are usually found, with walls probably being constructed from planks. These are sometimes indicated by trench foundations that held continuous upright timbers. The position of the door can be visible in the plan. At West Stow, one door was usually located in one long wall, but at Mucking, halls had two doors opposite each other in the long sides of the building. Of course, there is no indication of the number and position of windows. Shutters were probably used for these rather than glass (**53**). Evidence is occasionally found for internal divisions in the buildings. At Mucking, several had a partition at one end, interpreted as a store. There is also the possibility that a loft or mezzanine floor was incorporated into some, perhaps just for part of their length. This would give extra space for storage, or possibly even for sleeping if the upper level was not too smoky.

At West Stow, keys made of antler were discovered. These would have been inserted through a hole in the door and used to open or close an internal bolt (**colour plate 17**). Although such measures would not have stopped a determined burglar, a bolted door would have been a deterrent, especially against inquisitive children. Within a small community, such locks may have been particularly useful for stopping pilfering or unauthorised 'borrowing' from stores, rather like the modern office stationery cupboard. Iron latch lifters and keys are frequently found in female graves, again hinting at mechanisms used for fastening doors. Their association with women may indicate who was in charge of the home (**54**).

Hearths in the centre of the house provided heat and somewhere to cook, as well as a little light. Smoke would rise up into the rafters to drift out through the thatch and eaves. Presumably, the main source of illumination came from candles. Tallow was used for candles from prehistoric times. This substance is made from animal fat, boiled in water until the water has almost completely evaporated. This can be a dangerous process because the tallow is highly flammable. The candles themselves also smell rather unpleasant when they are burning, to the modern nose at least. Beeswax can also be used for candles but, in comparison to honey, wax is made in small amounts by bees. Early Anglo-Saxon communities may not have had access to sufficient quantities for candles.

55 *Two possible reconstructions of the Spong Hill chair.* Photograph by A. Kemp, courtesy of West Stow Village Trust/St Edmundsbury Borough Council

Furniture does not usually survive, but there are a number of clues as to what may have been used. A cremation urn from Spong Hill shows a man on what looks like a dining room chair with no arms. However, this is difficult to interpret and the chair may be a solid, throne-like item or a lighter stave built piece (**55**). Remains of beds have been found on a number of occasions in graves dating to the seventh century. Two examples from Edix Hill show that they could be sophisticated structures. It was not possible to reconstruct either completely, but components included a wooden frame made of ash, and other elements of metal, textile and leather. Each had a headboard. Leather straps in one may originally have supported the mattresses, but this was uncertain. Other Anglo-Saxon beds had wooden slats for a mattress to sit on. In *Beowulf*, the Lord Hrothgar sleeps on a private couch, while others make do with beds and bolsters brought out and put on the floor as the benches are cleared away.

Certain types of keys and lock mechanisms prove that valuables were kept in secure boxes. Tables, benches, shelves and chests probably also graced the Anglo-Saxon home, some of which may have been carved for decoration. Early English woodworking skills were considerable.

Soft furnishings do not survive but are likely to have been commonplace. *Beowulf* mentions pillows, wall-hangings and tapestries. As well as decorating homes, the latter would have had the added advantage of acting as draft excluders and insulation. However, making a wall hanging represents a significant investment in terms of time and raw materials, so it cannot be assumed that they would be available to every household. Conversely, once made they do not wear out, so could have been passed down through generations. Woven rugs are another possibility. There is no reason to think that people did not make the effort to ensure that their dwellings were as comfortable as possible.

The second type of building often found on settlement sites was generally smaller and constructed over a pit, usually with only two or six postholes surviving. Size, exact shape and construction vary considerably, perhaps indicating a wide range of functions. These are known as Grubenhäuser or Sunken Featured Buildings (SFBs) (**colour plate 20**). It is not known exactly how these appeared. Some have suggested that the pit is actually the floor surface, the building then only requiring low walls with the roof nearly reaching the ground. A door was situated in the gable end. A sunken floor would require steps leading down from the door and some measures might be needed to ensure it did not flood in bad weather. The pit walls would require revetment to prevent collapse. At Mucking, stake holes lining the pit were observed in several structures. Such buildings would be difficult to provide with windows and therefore would be rather gloomy. Others suggest that floorboards were inserted above the pit and the resulting structure could be used for many purposes including as a dwelling. This seems likely at West Stow where no evidence of supporting the pit sides was discovered.

It is difficult to be sure how roofs were constructed because no standing buildings survive from the pagan period. However, thatch seems likely. Alternatively, small wooden tiles called shingles could have been used. These may have been supported on curved wooden frames called crucks. SFBs usually out-number halls and many contain objects associated with various types of work, suggesting these were the utility buildings which would have been required on the settlement. At West Stow coprolites (preserved excrement) were found in some SFBs as well as in pits dating to the fifth and sixth centuries. It was not possible to determine whether this was animal or human, but the shape and inclusions suggest it was most likely to be pig or human. In two buildings, the coprolites were in distinct concentrations suggesting that if these were animal then the pigs were tethered, and if they were human, specific areas were designated for use, like a type of latrine. No evidence for 'toilet' structures is mentioned, but if these consisted of wooden seats with holes in, no trace would be likely to survive.

The pit over which SFBs were constructed often filled up after the building went out of use. This could be a gradual, natural process but there is evidence that the hollows were filled up deliberately by the community using them as rubbish pits. Remains of buildings also give important clues about carpentry. Planks used in buildings were thicker at one edge than the other.

This is because they were made by radially splitting the tree trunk rather than sawing it. Wooden or iron wedges were hammered into the timber, causing it to split along its length. Hence one edge of the plank came from the outer surface of the tree and the other from its centre. The framework for a building was probably constructed using joints and wooden pegs (trenails) to secure the timbers together. Houses may have been carved and painted for decoration, but evidence of this does not survive.

Hearths for cooking and heating occur in many structures. Obviously, these could not be made directly onto the wooden floor, but a box lined with clay or filled with sand will contain the fire adequately. Hearths were also made in the open air. Some of these were made directly onto the ground surface, but layers of clay were also used. At West Stow, one had a base of Roman tile and another of burnt clay and stones. When the weather allowed, people probably stayed outside as much as possible, cooking and eating in the open air. For many occupations, such as spinning, making pottery, bone and woodwork, natural light would be more pleasant and easier to work in than candle light.

Pits are common on settlement sites. Large examples, including a number from Eye Kettleby, were used for cooking. Cobbles were heated to a high temperature in a fire and then put into the bottom of the pit. Food was wrapped in coarse cloth and placed on the cobbles. A layer of earth capped the structure and the food roasted slowly. This method of cooking has the advantage that the heat source is contained, cannot pose a threat to the buildings, and can be left while everybody goes off and does something else. However, cooking in this way does require a significant amount of effort and perhaps was most frequently used at times of particular consequence, when a feast was appropriate, but the people wanted to participate in a communal activity.

Other pits can be circular, oval or square. Some were lined but their original purpose is unclear although grain and other foods can be stored in pits. Many were eventually filled with rubbish.

At Chalton in Hampshire, a complex of features was uncovered which provide a picture of a working Anglo-Saxon farm. There was a large rectangular building with a door in the middle of each long side which was the house. Joining onto the east end was an enclosure that contained two smaller buildings. These may have been workshops or stores. At Cowdrey Down, a similar arrangement of a house with an enclosure containing other buildings was also found. In addition, there was a large hall to the south. The entrance to such enclosures could be very narrow and it has been suggested that there may have been herb and vegetable gardens within. The narrow entrances were to prevent animals wandering in and causing damage.

Making clothes

Archaeological evidence provides us with many clues about textile production. Wool and linen were the main types of cloth made. Some breeds of sheep living at the time may have been plucked rather than shorn, like the Soay. Some cleaning would then be necessary. Wool was also combed to make the fibres lie in the same direction. At West Stow, iron points were found which were probably the teeth from such combs. The wool was then spun into yarn using a drop spindle. This is basically a stick with a circular weight near the lower tip.

The spindle was made from wood, so has usually rotted. The weight or whorl could be made from materials like bone, fired clay or even rock crystal which are much more likely to survive. The spindle was twisted between the fingers and thumb and as it revolved the fibres were fed through the other hand and so spun into thread. The threads could be spun clockwise, S-spun, or anti-clockwise, Z-spun. As well as wool, textiles were made of linen from flax.

Spinning seems to have been an important activity for women and spindle whorls are found in female graves, even those of the wealthy. They were the second most common object type on the settlement at West Stow. Most were ceramic, including ones made from pieces of Roman pots. Chalk, bone, shale, stone and lead were other materials used. The exact shape of the whorls could be assigned to eleven categories, which were all used throughout the fifth and sixth century. It has been estimated that about eight miles of thread was needed to produce a man's tunic. Anglo-Saxon women were probably faster than even the most adept modern spinners, but this still represents many hours work.

Yarn was made into cloth by weaving on a warp-weighted loom. Such looms were upright, but needed to lean at an angle, for example against a wall. The vertical threads, known as the warp, were held taut with clay loom weights (**56**). These were sometimes baked, but were often made simply from dried clay. As they would not be likely to get wet, firing was unnecessary and may have had the adverse affect of making them more brittle. Reconstructions show that fired loom weights break very easily, especially in contact with enthusiastic schoolchildren. The weights were often 'ring doughnut' (annular) in form, becoming more 'bun-shaped' as time progressed. The frame of the loom was made of wood and, therefore, does not survive on archaeological sites.

However, at some places such as West Stow, sets of loom weights have been found in positions corresponding to the original set up of the loom. In two instances, buildings had burnt down and the loom weights were left where they dropped. One SFB seems to have housed three looms, a small one with only 18 loom weights and two bigger ones with 60 and 90. This suggests that fabrics of contrasting widths were being made, probably for specific purposes. Many other structures contained a number of loom weights. It is likely that, where possible, looms were situated near doors to

56 *Clay loom weights. The yarn tied to them has begun to wear one away so its central perforation is no longer circular.* Photograph by A. Kemp, courtesy of Jewry Wall Museum, Leicester

maximise the light. At Mucking, 140 loom weights were discovered in one building. Although they were roughly in rows, the number found in relation to the space available implies that they were in storage rather than use. To make the horizontal weft threads lie neatly and closely together they were beaten up with a weaving batten, an object resembling a blunt sword. Iron examples are known from a few wealthy women's graves, but one was also recovered from a hall at West Stow.

Pin beaters are thought to be associated with weaving and are fairly common finds on settlement sites. They are made of bone, pointed at both ends and highly polished from use. They may have been used for moving uneven or protruding threads. However, when weaving tapestries the weft is beaten up in smaller sections at a time to create the pattern so perhaps pin beaters had a more specialised use.

The early Anglo-Saxons used various types of weave and it is not proposed to describe them in detail here. (See Owen-Crocker, G. 1986, *Dress in Anglo-Saxon England*). The type of weave used can in itself create a pattern in the fabric and tabby, twill, three shed twills and broken twills were all used. Three shed twills may be significant because they were used by the Romans, but were not used in Scandinavia, part of the Anglo-Saxon homelands, until Viking times. Their use by Anglo-Saxons has led to the suggestion that this is evidence of continuing Roman influence. They perhaps even used a type of

Roman loom, which did not use loom weights, but the warp was attached to a bar. Some cloth was woven with a Z-spun warp and an S-spun weft. This would also produce a pattern in the cloth. There is evidence of weaving cloth with stripes or checks. A piece of this was found on a brooch from the cemetery of Cleatham, Humberside.

Tablet weaving was a technique used to make decorative braids which were very strong and, therefore, also suitable for straps and belts. Square tablets with a hole at each corner were threaded with the warp (**colour plate 15**). The tablets were then turned forwards and backwards with the weft being passed through the warp at each turn. Repeating designs could be produced by completing a set number of turns forward and then the same back. Much more complex patterns could be made by varying the turning sequence or turning each card individually, some moving forwards as others were turned backwards. There is little evidence for the actual motifs used, but fragments suggest chevrons were one element. Gold foil was occasionally incorporated into the weaving, but this was very rare. Embroidery could have been added to the completed braid to give extra refinement to the detail. By the late Anglo-Saxon period, England was famous for its embroidery and this technique may have been used in its own right to decorate garments and soft furnishings.

Tablet woven braid could be produced using the tablets on their own or these could be incorporated onto a full size loom to produce a starting border. Two hole tablets were used for less decorative purposes. Tablet weaving was practised by the Iron Age Britons, Romans and Vikings as well as the Anglo-Saxons.

On Anglo-Saxon sites, the cloth itself rarely survives but a 'cast' of the threads can be preserved in the corrosion products of metal (**57**). This means that small 'fossils' of cloth can be found on metal items such as buckles, brooches and wrist clasps. These contain evidence about the production method of the fabric, such as the direction of spinning and the type of weaving. Fragments of cloth associated with wrist clasps show that tablet weaving was used to decorate the wrist of long-sleeved undergarments and to act as a type of cuff.

On rare occasions, pieces of the fabric itself survive and traces of pigments used on the cloth can be retrieved. This hints at the brightly coloured nature of Anglo-Saxon clothing. The cemetery of Fonaby in Lincolnshire yielded a high number of cloth samples. Blue-green threads were still visible on one brooch and blue or green and red or purple fibres were identified in a piece of tablet weaving. Many colours are available from natural dyes including yellow from onionskins or weld; blue from woad leaves; and red and orange from madder. Elderberry, lichen, fungus, damson and bark may also have been used (**colour plate 16**). Colours were probably associated with status. For example, woad produces blue, but darker shades require part of the dyeing process to be repeated. Other hues, including certain greens, are achieved by dyeing with first one colour and then another thus taking twice the materials

57 *As this shield boss fragment and brooch corroded, they preserved casts of pieces of cloth that were resting against them.* Photograph by A. Kemp, courtesy of Jewry Wall Museum, Leicester

and time. Another ingredient required by some dyes was an alkali, which could have been in the form of lime, but another readily available source was stale urine. Waste not, want not. Many natural dyes do not take unless the fabric is first treated with a mordant. Iron salts from rusty nails would be one type available to the earliest English. A range of shades, including dark ones, can be produced on wool but linen tends to colour to lighter, more pastel hues. As can be seen, dyeing was a complex process and achieving good results required skill and extensive knowledge. The different colours available naturally from wool could also be used decoratively in garments.

Needles are found on settlement sites. They were made of bone and were often chunky. However, judging by the fineness of thread that could be made, it seems logical that more delicate examples existed. Their small size would perhaps make them less likely to survive and would also make them harder for excavators to see and recover.

Evidence from graves shows that at least some processes of textile production, like spinning, were carried out by women. Adding all the stages together emphasises what a labour intensive activity making clothes and soft furnishings was. If women carried out dyeing, weaving, braid making and sewing, then these tasks must have filled a significant part of their working life. As a result, people probably had limited wardrobes and valued them highly. It seems likely that children would be taught to contribute from as early an age as possible, time being too precious a resource to waste even on the young.

Producing pottery

Pottery was used for many purposes, including drinking and eating, storage, cooking and for burying the cremated remains of the dead (**58**). Not surprisingly then, pots come in many shapes and sizes to suit the variety of uses. From an archaeological point of view, it has the added advantage of surviving when buried in the ground.

To modern eyes, early Anglo-Saxon pottery appears crude. It is not symmetrical and the shape of one side of a pot can differ dramatically from the opposite side. Lines incised around a vessel as decoration may not join up. However, this apparent 'lack of skill' and these 'mistakes' could have been rectified relatively easily when the clay was still in its plastic state. The fact that changes were not made suggests that the finished product was quite satisfactory for early English tastes and in truth, some of it at least, would require a great deal of skill to make (**colour plate 22**). It has been argued that pottery for everyday use was made at home but that professional potters made some special vessels. There is no evidence to suggest whether or not pottery production was the preserve of one gender.

On the western edge of the settlement at West Stow, there was a roughly circular ditched enclosure that contained a thick, irregular layer of clay. This is thought to have been a clay reserve. In medieval times, after it had been dug

58 *Small, plain pots which may have been used as cups.* Photograph by A. Kemp, courtesy of Jewry Wall Museum, Leicester

from pits or riverbanks, clay was left exposed to the elements over winter. The clay weathered down and large impurities, like stones, came to the surface and were easier to remove.

The early Anglo-Saxons did not use a potter's wheel. For small vessels, thumb or pinch pots were adequate. These were made by rolling clay into a ball, inserting the thumb into its centre and pinching the clay to the desired shape while slowly turning the ball. Larger pots were coil built. 'Sausages' of clay were built up in layers to make the sides of the pot. While the clay was still soft, each coil was smoothed into the other until they were no longer visible.

A great deal of pottery was left plain. However, a substantial variety of decorative techniques were available to the potter. These could be used singly or in almost any combination. Incised or scored lines were a common motif. They were often used horizontally, around the neck or shoulders of the pot, but also vertically and can even be found on the base of vessels. Shallower, softer impressed lines were also utilised and impressed dots were a common design, often in groups. Many objects could have been used for making lines and dots. However, at West Stow, bone implements with rounded ends but no obvious function were found which would have been perfect for the job.

More complex designs were made with stamps (**colour plate 21**). A great variety was available from simple circles to runes and stylised animals. A number of stamps were often used on the same pot. The stamps were made from antler. A piece near the end of a prong, or tine, was cut off giving a roughly circular surface on which the motif could be carved. Five have been found in buildings at West Stow, confirming the pottery was made and decorated on the farmstead. Another stamp was discovered close by in a cremation urn at Illington. Unfortunately, the gender of the deceased could not be determined. Other items, such as decorative parts of brooches were also used to create designs in the soft clay. It has been suggested that the stamps used on cremation urns were more than just decorative. Particular patterns or groups may have been restricted to certain families.

Raised lumps or bosses were frequently added to vessels, usually for decoration. Extra pieces of clay could be moulded onto the vessel and smoothed in, or bosses could be pushed out from the body while the clay was still moist. Pierced bosses and larger lugs were functional, allowing the pot to be suspended, perhaps for cooking over a fire. The rim may also be specially shaped and pierced for the same purpose. Rusticated pottery was also made. Here the outer surface of the pot has been made rough by pinching with the thumb and fingers.

Early Anglo-Saxon pottery does not have the shiny, glassy glaze that we are used to seeing on almost all modern material. However, the surface was frequently rubbed very smooth or burnished. This would be done while the pot was drying out. The finished product would then have a shiny surface, but would also be stronger because burnishing compresses the clay particles.

A pot would probably have been left to dry for several days. To make it hard enough to use, it would need to be fired (basically 'cooked' at a high temperature for a long time). Any moisture left in the clay would cause it to break during firing. The Anglo-Saxons did not use kilns as the Romans before them had. They used controlled bonfires known as clamps to fire their pottery. A pit was dug in the ground and filled with dry urns and fuel. Turf was placed over the top to ensure the fire would burn slowly. It was also important to allow the pots to cool gradually because a fast drop in temperature would cause them to shatter.

Clamp firing did not produce such high temperatures as a kiln so the finished product was not as hard as Roman or medieval pottery. Therefore, it is more likely to disintegrate in the ground, making it harder for archaeologists to find. The distribution of oxygen in the bonfire is uneven. Some areas will be rich in oxygen, but others will be starved. This affects the colour of the clay and pots are often patchy, varying from black to orange.

Working with metals

Metalwork was also carried out on settlements. A variety of raw materials and techniques were utilised. However, one of the main properties of metal objects is that they can be melted down and reused especially if they are worn out or broken. This again means that there is less for the archaeologist to find.

Iron working debris is relatively common and this is not surprising bearing in mind the tools needed on a daily basis. Chopping axes, chains, hammers, cooking vessels and many other things were probably an everyday sight on a farmstead, but only rarely survive. Knives, shears, scythes and ploughshares were all essential farming equipment made from iron, but it was also the material of weapons such as spearheads, shield bosses, throwing axes and swords.

Small amounts of steel were made and this was sometimes added as an edge to iron blades as it could be sharpened more than iron and would not blunt as quickly. Knife blades were also hardened or tempered by treating them with fire (Timby, J. 1996). Occasionally, very sophisticated techniques were employed including pattern welding. This process was used to make blades from many rods of metal twisted together and beaten out repeatedly. The resulting blade was very strong, but also had a very distinctive appearance. Traces of the rods could be seen on the surface producing rippled, wavy patterns.

Metals made by combining a selection from copper, lead, zinc or tin are called copper alloys, and include bronze and brass. These were used for jewellery and dress fittings including brooches, buckles, girdle hangers and tweezers (tweezers were also made from iron). Copper alloys are suitable for decorative items because they could be cast in moulds incorporating the main elements of a design, but then be further worked using, for example, punches. However, the items are also strong enough to be used for practical purposes. At Mucking, evidence of the actual production of copper alloy jewellery survives, which is not common. A fragment of a sixth-century saucer brooch appears to be from a failed casting. More unusual still was the discovery of fragments of a two-piece mould for a square-headed brooch. Part of both the front and the back section survived and the mould was made from sandy, fired clay. This may have been encased in a fresh layer of clay to hold both parts securely together when the molten metal was poured in. There is some evidence that the particular mix of copper alloy was carefully selected for its particular properties depending on the item being made. For example, zinc-rich brasses were used for sheet metal because they were more malleable (can be worked and bent).

Analysis of the copper alloys from Empingham II showed that some pairs of objects, including girdle hangers and some brooches, were of identical composition, presumably because they were made at the same time. However, relatively few items seemed to come from the same batch of metal,

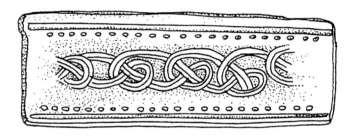

59 *Gold foil was rubbed against a die, like this one from Leicestershire, to emboss it with a design (5cm long).* Drawn by R. Knox

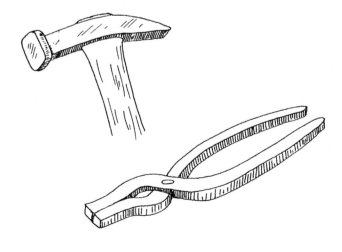

60 *Hammers and tongs, like those from Tattershall Thorpe, Lincolnshire, were used by metal workers.* Redrawn by R. Knox from Hinton

61 *Wayland the Smith, from A. W. Frank's Casket, holds tongs in one hand and stands behind an anvil block.* Drawn by R. Knox

which indicated production on a small scale. Some metals seem to be melted down Roman ones, but small amounts of nickel and arsenic in others suggest fresh production.

Gold and silver were both used by the Anglo-Saxons. Precious metals impressed with intricate patterns were used on objects including drinking horns (**59**). Occasionally, brooches were made from silver and decorated with gold (**colour plate 23**). Both were used as surface decoration on objects made of cheaper metals such as copper alloy. Gold foil was also used in textiles in Kent. The metal was incorporated into the braid as it was woven. Such gold braids were used in headdresses. Gold was also used in beads encased in glass. Presumably, this gave the maximum appearance for the minimum amount of metal. The glass also protected the soft gold.

Tools for working wood and metal were not usually placed in graves, but one exception was found at Tattershall Thorpe in Lincolnshire (Hinton, D. A. 2000). This grave, dating from around AD 660-70, contained so many tools and pieces of scrap metal that it is thought to be the grave of a smith. A number of hammers were found (**60**). These came in different sizes, suggesting they had different purposes. They would be appropriate for general wood and metalworking, but it is suggested that one of the small hammers was particularly suited to beating out copper alloy sheet or shaping wire. An anvil and tongs with snub-nosed jaws and traces of wood on the long handles were discovered. These would have been used for metalworking, as seen on a carved panel showing Weland (Wayland) the Smith on the Frank's casket (**61**). This box made of bone dates to the eighth century, but the basic smithing principals are unlikely to have changed. Snips, a plate for drawing wire, punches and files were just some of the other tools found (**62**). Some, at least, had wooden handles as the burin or scriber with a boxwood handle demonstrates. This shows that a wide range of tools was available to the Anglo-Saxon craftsman. Many of these would be recognised by wood and metalworkers today.

Copper alloy, lead, gold and silver were all found as scrap. Fragments of glass and cut garnets were also placed in the grave. The smith was probably keeping these things so they could be melted down to make new items, or to repair old ones. These materials for recycling and his tool kit suggest the man may have specialised in iron and jewellery.

He may have been an itinerant worker if there was not sufficient demand in one place for his skills. One of the objects found with the smith was a bell. King Wihtred's Law Code of AD 695 states that if a traveller or foreigner strayed from the path without shouting or blowing his horn he could be assumed to be a thief so could be killed. Perhaps the smith used his bell to announce his presence (Hinton, D. A. 2000).

Materials from animals

Bone and antler were versatile materials used for a large range of items from combs to gaming pieces, and from spindle whorls to pottery stamps. They were the Anglo-Saxon equivalent to plastic. At Mucking, a ditch was found which contained substantial quantities of antler. This was probably a deliberate deposit because antler is easier to work with after soaking. Sawn antler was recovered from one building confirming the material was used on site. A large quantity of material was retrieved from West Stow (**colour plate 24**). Combs were made on the site and unfinished examples were discovered. Fine saws, drills, clamps and scribing tools would all have been needed for the job, but tools themselves rarely survive. Long fragments of bone for items like needles were obtained by grooving and splitting bones.

Horn was another important raw material and was often used for knife handles. Spong Hill settlement produced horn sawn from a sheep's skull, indicating that work was carried out on site.

Leather was a crucial product. Cattle bones from Spong Hill farmstead had knife cuts consistent with skinning the carcass. This was carried out with skill and care, including removing the hide from the lower legs, which were more

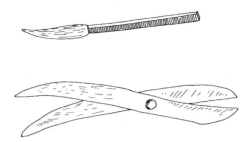

62 *Snips and files were also found at Tattershall Thorpe.* Redrawn by R. Knox from Hinton

frequently discarded (Rickett, R. 1995). There are a number of methods for preparing leather. Once removed from the animal, the fatty layer beneath the skin has to be scraped off. The hair also needs to be removed and again can be scraped off, but the task is easier if the hide is soaked in urine because the hair begins to decay. The remaining leather will go stiff and may rot unless treated further. Smoking over a slow burning fire and then rubbing in an oil dressing of egg yolk, tallow or cattle brains will give a temporary stable result. However, decay will eventually set in especially if the leather gets wet. Tanning gives a more permanent result.

Preferably, the pelt needs to be swelled before tanning. In effect, this is achieved by partial rotting, a process which is encouraged by bacteria from dung and dog excrement. Hides were then soaked in a tan bath. Tannin was obtained from woods like oak and larch. The exact type used affects the colour of the leather. Oil dressings were probably applied after tanning to keep the leather supple. Finer grades tend to come from smaller animals like sheep and goats or young beasts, such as calves (Hodges, H. 1976).

Farming and food

The early Anglo-Saxons were self-sufficient in most things. All they needed could be grown or found in the countryside around them, but this meant working life was inextricably linked to the seasons. Evidence excavated from their settlements and cemeteries gives clues to the crops that were grown and foods that were eaten. Later Anglo-Saxon writings suggest how these foods were preserved and cooked, although there is always the possibility that some changes had occurred over time.

Some areas were made into fields for growing crops. Roman fields were probably reused in certain cases. A type of plough more able to cope with heavy clay soils came into more regular use in the Anglo-Saxon period, so more land could have been brought into cultivation. Later documents show oxen pulling the plough with a boy using a goad in front and a man guiding the plough behind. Some crops, such as rye were probably sown in the autumn, but most ploughing would be a winter activity which was a hard, physical job when the weather was likely to be at its worst. The Anglo-Saxons called February 'mud month'. Even in much later times ploughing was not an easy activity. One folk song from the nineteenth century refers to 'the painful plough'. Sowing was predominantly a spring occupation. Another pleasant job would be manuring the fields to help preserve their fertility. Domestic and animal refuse was probably saved and spread over fields.

Summer was harvest time. In the long, hot days, probably in July, the grass from meadows was cut and dried to make hay for winter animal fodder. A wet summer could be disastrous because it could destroy a crop and leave nothing to feed the beasts on. In more recent times, around a tonne was needed per head of cattle, but allowing for the fact that Anglo-Saxon breeds were smaller, it can be suggested that they required about half a tonne per animal. This still represents many hours of exhausting, backbreaking work. Space was also needed to stack the hay in until it was used, preferably inside. If hay is not dried properly, a stack can begin to heat up and even spontaneously combust, so it is likely that regular checks would be made to ensure this did not occur.

Cereals were also harvested around this time of year. Bede records that the Anglo-Saxon name for August was 'weed month'. Farmers would attempt to ensure that their crops were ripe before the weeds developed and contaminated them. In some cases, the arable fields may have been weeded by hand. Even today, farmers who choose not to use herbicides remove weeds such as wild oats by hand (pers. comm. H Hollingsworth). Reaping hooks are among the agricultural equipment found on farms. Some are relatively small and may have been more suited to cutting bunches of plant material rather than an arable crop. Tools for cutting all crops were probably made of iron rather than steel, which was only available in small quantities. Harvesting was, therefore, even more laborious because it would be necessary to stop frequently to re-sharpen the blade, as iron will not retain a good edge for long. When reaping was complete, grain still needed to be separated from the chaff before it could be used. Residues from such processing are found on settlement sites.

Burnt grains and impressions of grain in pottery from sites around the country show that barley, bread wheat, spelt, oats and rye were all grown. The exact proportions and combinations would be dictated by local conditions. Rye was found at West Stow and is particularly adaptable to its sandy soils, but oats require damper conditions and may have been imported into the site. Wheat, barley, oats and rye were used to make bread, although wheat was preferred because it makes a lighter, more airy loaf. Barley bread is heavier and more strongly flavoured (Hagen, A. 1992). Hand mills or querns for grinding the grain into flour have been discovered at a number of settlement sites. Anglo-Saxon querns were made of two large, round and relatively flat stones. The upper stone had a hole in the centre into which grain was poured. This trickled down between the stones, the top stone was rotated and the grain was crushed between the stones with the flour spilling out over the edge.

A deposit of rye at West Stow seems to have been ready for sowing or processing, but another batch was burnt. Closer examination suggests that this may have been a deliberate action because the crop was contaminated with seeds from a weed called corn cockle. This taints the flour and is also toxic. Rye can also be affected by ergot, which develops particularly in wet springs. This contamination can cause gangrene and miscarriages. It has also been linked to symptoms of hallucinations and convulsions which have been attributed to acts of witchcraft in more recent cultures, including the witch trials in Salem, America.

Weeds in the crop were not always harmful and in some cases could even have enhanced the flavour. Archaeologically, they are important because specific species indicate the type of landscape they grew in. At West Stow, weeds show that well drained soil near the settlement was under cultivation, but this was supplemented by working more poorly drained areas. Eye Kettleby in Leicestershire had disturbed as well as fully arable land in its vicinity, with pollen evidence also suggesting a largely open and inhabited landscape rather than, for example, a heavily wooded one.

Barley had other important uses as well as for bread. Just like today, it was probably added to stews to give thickness and bulk. It was also used to make ale. Oats may have been used for porridge-type dishes as well as pottage and stew. Vegetables were important foodstuffs which were perhaps grown in plots close to or within the settlement. Although the names of many of these are familiar to us, Anglo-Saxon varieties probably looked quite different. For example, orange carrots were introduced in post-medieval times. Celery, radishes, parsnips, peas, beans, onions, leek and beets were all available in some form.

Animals provided meat, milk and dairy produce, wool, leather, transport and a power source for the plough. Caring for them was another crucial task. The later Anglo-Saxon medical text, *Lacnunga*, contains cures for livestock as well as people. Sheep, pigs and cattle are all specifically mentioned, but the greatest number of animal cures refers to the horse. Perhaps this is indicative of the animal's status. Most of the remedies combine prayers, holy water and herbs. However, in some instances it is difficult to feel optimistic about the probable result. One cure for a rash on a horse included making the poor beast stand in running water whilst you sang into its ear.

Milk from cows, sheep and goats could be drunk, but full cream milk may have been a luxury. Whey skimmed milk and buttermilk can be used for drinking after the milk has been used for cream, butter and cheese. A number of types of cheese were probably available. Some may have hung in the rafters to protect them from vermin. They would be smoked as a result by the open fire or hearth in the centre of the hall. Hard, soft and perhaps even blue cheese may all have been made. Mature cheeses were probably restricted to the well off because they would have to have enough surplus to leave it for a long time before eating and because it also needed more salt as a preservative (Hagen, A. 1992).

In some regions, sheep were probably moved to upland pasture in the summer and returned to the lowland in the autumn and winter. Lambing in spring must have been as busy a time then as it is now. Later Anglo-Saxon documents describe the shepherd milking, making butter and cheese as well as protecting the sheep. At West Stow, four large hollows may indicate the positions of animal pens but no trace of fences around them survived. Sheep and goats, cattle, pigs and occasionally horses were eaten. Animal bones frequently show cut marks associated with butchery. Bones from the settlement at Spong Hill indicate heavy chopping blows to dismember the carcass. Marks on cattle jaws suggest the tongues, a valuable source of meat, were removed. As well as providing food, fat could be made into tallow candles.

Ducks, chickens and geese were kept. Eggs were found in a burial at Great Chesterford. Feathers were probably not wasted because they could have been used to stuff cushions and pillows. In addition, they were needed as fletchings for arrows.

Honey was a vital sweetening agent which may have been collected from the wild. Once the location of a nest was known, it would be possible to cut a door in the tree trunk and return regularly to collect more honey. However, considering the importance of honey it seems likely that the early Anglo-Saxons would have taken measures to ensure they had a continued supply. Simple hives could be made from logs or bark and kept on the settlement. As long as honey was harvested and the weather remained favourable, the bees would continue to produce more. However, such hives leave no archaeological trace (Hagen, A. 1995). The honey is sealed into the comb by a layer of wax. This would have been useful in its own right, perhaps as a sealant for foodstuffs stored in jars.

Certain foods became plentiful at particular times of the year, for example fruits and vegetables. Meat supplies probably reflected seasonal circumstances. To ensure there was enough food all year round, methods for preserving it were needed. Salt was added to cheese, meat and butter as a preservative. Drying, smoking, pickling and boiling may also have been used. Other methods included storage jars made airtight with clarified butter as well as separate store buildings away from the heat of the hall. These provisions would help feed the people through the year, but diet would still vary on a seasonal basis.

In winter the diet probably consisted of bread, salt meat, legumes and cheese with some leeks. Some varieties of cabbage, leeks and onions are available early on and lamb may have been available in spring. However, it must be remembered that spring comes much later to some parts of the country than others. What was available in the south might have been different from what was available in the Peak District or the north.

In the summer and autumn, nuts and fruits would be readily available, possibly eaten with cream. There may have been shortages in the early summer as old supplies ran out before the harvest. Mutton became available, but animals slaughtered in the summer would be likely to go off quickly. In later times, it became the custom never to eat pork in the summer because this goes off more quickly than other meats (Hagen, A. 1992). Therefore, it was probably saved for the autumn. Livestock kept over winter would have to be fed so decisions may have been made at this time of year about what would be needed. Any surplus would probably be killed, but there is no evidence of a mass autumn slaughter. Milk, ale, wines, cider, mead and water could all be drunk with meals.

No cookery books survive from early Anglo-Saxon times, but some later writings give clues to what may have been eaten. Leechdoms, books primarily connected with medicine, mention chicken stewed with wine, beef marinated in vinegar and oil made into a broth with dill and leeks (Hagen, A. 1992).

As in the Second World War, most early Anglo-Saxons probably 'ate what they'd got'. Food could come from the farm, the wood, the river or the sea. The hearth is the central feature of many Anglo-Saxon halls and it is easy to imagine a cooking pot over it, steaming away day after day with any available vegetables, meat and herbs being thrown in. Stew (rather than spam) was the order of the day. Societies past and present need times to celebrate and so there were probably feast days when more varieties of foods were provided. Not everybody would have eaten the same things. There are always those who are more important or wealthier who get the best of everything and food would be no exception.

Preparing, storing and deciding what and how much food to eat through the year would have taken a great deal of skill, time and effort. Seeds for the next year's crops needed to be kept safe. Supplies required continuous monitoring to ensure they had not become contaminated or infested. The lives of the community literally depended on it.

Living off the land

Woodland provided many important resources. Early Anglo-Saxons used timber for building rather than stone. In addition, fences, carts, furniture, bowls and buckets are just some of the items that would be common in a settlement but rarely survive on archaeological sites. Coal was used a little by the Romans and was known to the Anglo-Saxons so was probably used in some areas, but wood was still the major fuel for cooking and heating as well as for working metal and glass, and firing pottery. In some areas, cremation was the predominant funerary rite and placed another demand on timber resources. Some woodland management, at least, took place in the form of coppicing. Particular tree types were cut off at ground level. The resulting stump then re-grows multiple shoots. When these had grown to the required height or thickness, sometimes after many years, they were cut off and the process began again. Ash and hazel grow long, straight poles that were used for spear shafts; traces of both have been found in iron spear sockets. These coppiced woods are also excellent for fencing. Poles were charred as a way of preserving them and a late Anglo-Saxon manuscript, the Cotton Tiberius calendar, shows this as a job for November. Timber was so important that by the seventh century at least, it was protected by law. The codes of King Ine for Wessex included measures to protect trees from destruction by fire and unauthorised felling. Woodland management emphasises not only the skill of the Anglo-Saxons but highlights their need for long term planning in order to survive and thrive. Did the first settlers look for Roman managed woodland which they could take over, or select new areas, knowing that it would be a number of years before they could reap their first harvest?

Wooden vessels which were beginning to break or split were sometimes repaired with copper alloy. Some were buried in graves and over the centuries, as the cup or bowl decayed, metal corrosion products preserved enough wood to allow the species to be determined. At the cemetery of Sewerby, six vessels were found and the wood of five was identified. These were wild cherry, ash, chestnut, maple and beech. The remains of at least four boxes were found in a seventh century grave at Tattershall Thorpe. One of these was made of lime, another was probably oak. The boxes had metal fittings and one may have had a curved top (Hinton, D.A. 2000). Tools with wooden handles were also found. One hammer had an ash handle, which would have been good for absorbing the shock of the hammer blows, and a piercer had a boxwood handle suitable for withstanding pressure and percussion. The fact that so many different woods were used suggests that the Anglo-Saxons were skilled at making the most of the raw materials around them.

Woods and forests provided a further source of meat to the hunter. Deer and badger have been found at excavated sites including Mucking and West Stow. Berries, fruits and nuts were gathered. Woodland provided food for animals. During the late summer and autumn, pigs could be allowed to forage for fodder such as acorns and although it is more unusual cattle, horses and sheep can take advantage of this seasonal pasture. However, if the area was being managed to grow fence poles and so forth then pollarding may have been necessary to prevent the animals grazing too heavily on the trees. This was similar to coppicing, but the trunk was left untouched to between 6ft and 15ft above the ground, and was cut at this level. Poles then grew from the elevated stump and could be harvested repeatedly. Pollarding is a tricky business because it requires sawing while standing on a ladder and it was probably not undertaken unless absolutely necessary (Rackham, O. 1990). Perhaps some of the injuries mentioned in chapter 3 were sustained during attempted pollarding.

As mentioned above there is evidence that clothes could be brightly coloured and plants were the source for many of these dyes. Wetlands, marsh and water were other areas rich in resources. Reeds could be used for thatching roofs and possibly for rush lights. Meadows may have been mown to provide fodder for animals.

Water is perhaps the most crucial resource a community needs. It is also very heavy and cumbersome to carry so settlements were probably situated as close as possible to a suitable source. As well as drinking water for humans and animals, it was needed for cooking, brewing and more 'industrial' processes including dyeing, making pottery and metalworking. In addition, streams and rivers provided fish and waterfowl. Pike, perch, crane and swan were found at West Stow. Nets and rods could have been used for fishing, but more sophisticated and intensive methods were employed, namely the construction of fish weirs. These wickerwork or net traps had the advantage of being able to be left unattended with fish being collected from them at intervals. Hurdles or brushwood structures were inserted into the river or stream to guide the fish towards the weir. Similar traps were used on mud flats and in the sea. Fish weirs have been found dating back to the seventh century (Hagen, A. 1995), but there is no reason why they should not have been used earlier. The scale of fishing was probably dependant on the size and needs of the community as well as the abundance of fish. If circumstances were favourable some of the catch was probably preserved and traded. In Essex, fishing was intensive with weirs incorporating wattle walkways so that fish could be collected and repairs made without the fisherman sinking into the mud (*British Archaeology 41* 1999). Later Anglo-Saxon sources say that constructing fish weirs was a summer task, probably because river water was low and slower making it easier to work in. The early English also exploited the sea. However, consumption of marine fish was not restricted to the coast, bones being discovered at the settlement of Eye Kettleby in Leicestershire. These had probably been salted to preserve them. Foodstuffs other than fish were collected from the seashore. Mussels, periwinkles, limpets and oysters all seem to have been eaten. In later Saxon times, it is known that shellfish were transported many miles inland, oysters being kept alive in barrels of saltwater. Today, these are a delicacy but it is likely that in Anglo-Saxon times, before over-fishing, they were much more abundant and therefore available to a wider section of society.

What picture, then, can be built up of the settlements and daily activities of the earliest English? Farmsteads must have been very busy places with everyone from the very young to the old having a part to play. As well as seasonal work, such as lambing and harvesting, there would have been the never-ending tasks of feeding people and animals. Work spaces would have been required for a vast range of activities: making leather, dyeing cloth and butchering to name but a few. Taking these in combination with animal manure; fires for heating and cooking; furnaces for metalwork and decomposing heaps of rubbish destined for the fields, it seems likely that while Anglo-Saxon homes may have been warm and comfortable, parts of the settlements themselves stank to high heaven.

6 Rest and relaxation

Repetitive, physical labour was a major component of everyday life. Work was unremitting. Animals and crops could not be left to their own devices for long. In today's British society most people are fortunate enough to take holidays for granted. To our Anglo-Saxon antecedents, the thought of a fortnight's repose in the south of Gaul would have been a completely alien concept. However, people still needed to relax and unwind. Games, music, poetry, story-telling and sport are all recreational activities popular today which would have been familiar to the earliest English.

Games

We know that the early Anglo-Saxons played games because gaming pieces are found on settlements and in cremation urns. They were made from a variety of materials including bone, antler, horse teeth and natural pebbles. Roman coins may have been used in the settlements at West Stow and Eye Kettleby. Gaming pieces tend to be circular with a slightly domed top. Holes in the base of examples of antler and bone suggest they were made on a lathe. By examining the pieces and the contexts in which they appear, is it possible to deduce what actual games were being played?

The cremation cemetery at Spong Hill has produced over 2000 urns, 54 of which contained gaming pieces. The most common number per pot was one, which suggests a pastime of limited interest! However, the largest quantity found was over 31. Between these extremes there is no discernible 'usual' number. Many show evidence of burning, so it is probable that they were not all collected from the site of the pyre for interment. An extra complication with those made of bone is that burning would cause them to deform and in some cases fragment. It would then be difficult to separate them out from other small fragments of animal and human bone. Indeed, it is likely that in other, less thoroughly examined cremation collections some playing counters have gone undetected. Playing pieces are usually all the same colour although it must have been possible to tell each set apart when they were originally used. Bone pieces may have been painted, but paint does not survive and so it is uncertain how many counters each player controlled. However, different materials could be utilised for each side as at Caistor-by-

Norwich where one urn contained 33 pieces, 11 black, possibly made from shale (a type of soft rock) and 22 white, probably made from bone.

Many modern board games, like Monopoly, require dice to tell the player how far to move. Bone dice occur in Britain from the Iron Age and are common in Roman times. However, Anglo-Saxon dice are rare. Two bone examples, with 46 playing pieces, were found at Keythorpe Hall in Leicestershire. Two were again discovered together at Gilton near Sandwich and a clay cube from a burial at Alton in Hampshire may have originally been painted up as a die (**63**). It is possible that they were more common than the evidence suggests especially if they were predominantly made of wood. However, because they are so rare but there are two sites where pairs occur, this suggests at least one game requiring multiple dice was being played in the period. The boards themselves were probably carved in wood although it is possible that they could have been marked out on cloth or leather. None of these materials survive.

The remaining artefacts described above suggest the existence of board games using up to 46 pieces, possibly more. Dice were needed for some but not others. Although this is very little to go on, there are a number of games known from antiquity that fit the criteria. Nine Men's Morris is a very old game, which was played in Ancient Egypt and through the Roman period. It uses a board made up of three squares, one within another. There are two players who each have nine men that they take in turns to place on the board. When they are all down the men can then be moved with the aim of forming rows of three. Each time a row is made, one of the opponent's pieces is removed. This continues until one person has only two counters left or is hedged in and unable to move. As with many similar activities Nine Men's Morris can take minutes to learn and years to master. It still survives today, sometimes with its medieval name, Merrels.

A second game, which does not require dice, is hnefatafl (**64**). This also has a modern variation known as Fox and Geese. Hnefatafl was being played in Demark in AD 400 and so could easily have been brought to Britain by Anglian and Jutish settlers. It is a game of unequal sides. One has a king, and, in modern versions, 12 men but the other side has 24 men and no king. The larger side hunts the king and wins by blocking him in on all four sides.

63 *Dice are rare. This example, along with the gaming pieces, came from Keythorpe Hall in Leicestershire.* Drawn by R. Knox

64 *Playing board games seems to have been popular in Anglo-Saxon times.* Photograph by
A. Kemp, courtesy of West Stow Village Trust/St Edmundsbury Borough Council

However, if the king can reach one of the designated safe squares his side is victorious. The set of 33 coloured pieces from Caistor, mentioned above, follows the same proportions as the modern game and the possibility that this was a hnefatafl set is supported by another item in the urn, a roe deer ankle bone (astragalus). This bone may have been the king because it was brown, a different colour again, and had a runic inscription on one face.

Other ancient games needed dice, such as duodecim scripta, a Roman game reminiscent of backgammon. There were two players each with 15 counters. These were moved around the board in opposite directions. Players aimed to knock off their opponent's counters while ensuring their own reached safe spaces. Three dice were used to determine how far a player moved in a turn.

It is likely that versions of these games and others were known to the earliest English. If the game itself was not enough, extra excitement may have been created by placing bets. However, as they did not use coinage for money, perhaps possessions or services may have been wagered instead. As well as those mentioned above, sheep's astragali were probably used as gaming pieces. At Spong Hill, over 17 were found in one cremation, but when only one or two are recovered it is difficult to know whether they were playthings or part of a food offering.

123

Gaming pieces are found in cremations of both men and women. Most occur with mature adults, but children as young as about eight and older people over 40 were also given them as grave goods.

Songs and stories

Music is profound. It can affect moods and create emotions. This means that as well as bringing great joy or comfort to people, it can be used to manipulate them. Today, advertisers use jingles to make sure we remember the name of a product; patriotic sentiments are stirred by national anthems and the rendition of *Swing Low, Sweet Chariot* at an England rugby match instils a sense of comradeship in the supporters and inspires the players to strive for victory. Music is used to express celebration and mourning both today and by our Anglo-Saxon predecessors.

Sadly, it is not possible to recreate individual works of music from the period. If they were ever written down, it was not in a form that has survived. Many types of musical instrument such as drums and pipes may have existed but they would have been made of materials such as wood and skin, which are not preserved in normal circumstances. A bone object from Bury St Edmunds may have been a whistle but this is not certain. War horns are mentioned in poems, suggesting something that was usually used to convey orders or rally warriors, although they may have had a more musical function too. They are shown in later manuscripts being played alongside other instruments (**colour plate 26**).

However, evidence does survive for one early Anglo-Saxon musical instrument of some sophistication. A number of lyres or harps have been recovered from burials, ranging from the ship burial of a high king at Sutton Hoo to an otherwise humble grave at Bergh Apton, Norfolk. Where it has been possible to tell, harps were interred with men. The surviving harps tend to be in a fragmentary state, just a few tell-tale pieces surviving in a grave at Morning Thorpe, but an eighth-century manuscript, the Canterbury Psalter, shows one being played. The instrument is a rounded rectangular shape and has six strings. It is resting on the player's lap and he uses both hands to pluck the strings. A seventh-century example from Buckland was about two feet long and made of yew. This, and the one from Bergh Apton, had a strap that would be used to hold the instrument while keeping both hands free to play. There is an opening in the upper part of the harp so the strings cannot be pressed against a fingerboard as on a guitar or violin. This means that the only notes easily playable are those that the strings are tuned to, six in total. Most melodies use more and eight are needed for a whole scale. It is still possible to play a tune, but it is limited. The harp could be made more versatile by plucking two strings at once to accompany a melody that was being sung.

Harps were used by professional poet-musicians called scops (pronounced 'shops') who would perform to the assembled company in a lord's hall. Although purely instrumental pieces were possible, it is likely that harps were most often used by the scop to accompany himself as he recited or sang poetry, 'the song swelling to the sweet touched harp' (*Widsith*).

A poet would memorise and recite old works but needed to be able to compose new ones spontaneously at the request of his lord. As early Anglo-Saxon society was not literate, as we understand it, there were no means of writing a work down and committing it to memory when it was complete. To enable the scop to create on demand, poetry was produced to a formula that used specific patterns of stressed words. The ends of lines did not rhyme but certain words had to alliterate, which gave the verse a rhythm, helping the composer to retain a flow and momentum. For example, 'flushed with wine pride, flashing war gear' (*The Ruin*). Another useful tool was a collection of stock phrases, which occur with minor variations in many works.

It is likely that a poem was never performed the same way twice, but would be adapted to suit the mood and the individuals in the audience. After the conversion to Christianity, versions of some works were recorded in writing. Many surviving examples date to around AD 1000 and, strictly speaking, lie beyond the period under consideration, although some originated hundreds of years before. The surviving poems tend to have been written down by Christian monks who did not approve of their ancestors' pagan origins. This creates the additional problem that they seem to have introduced their own sections and quite possibly left out others. What survives is still a useful tool when trying to illuminate this elusive aspect of early Anglo-Saxon life.

Some of the surviving poems give us an insight into the life of a scop. Not every settlement could afford a professional entertainer so the patronage and protection of a wealthy lord was essential. The poem *Deor* tells of a poet who served a lord for many years, receiving rich rewards. However, he loses his home and his position when a more skilful poet arrives on the scene and displaces him. Widsith is another scop who has travelled through many lands because, 'The makar's weird is to be a wanderer'. In return for supporting a scop the lord could expect that, 'Lasting honour shall be his, / A name that shall never die beneath the heavens'. The lord becomes immortal, his prestige and glory will be remembered through the poems and songs that will outlast him. Considering these works have been preserved for more than a thousand years, Widsith was right. Widsith himself also seems to act as a sort of ambassador and public relations officer, accompanying a Lombard princess on her journey to marry Eomanric the Goth. Both these poems imply that a scop could be a valued and important member of a household, but their position was precarious and competed for.

The stories and poems themselves suggest that the earliest English had fertile imaginations and relished a good yarn. Many myths and legends are referred to which were common knowledge at the time but now survive only as fragments. Perhaps the most famous poem is *Beowulf*. The version that survives was written down about AD 1000 but is set in southern Scandinavia in the fifth and sixth centuries. It is an action adventure, which pits a super-human warrior against monsters and a dragon, but culminates in betrayal. Other works such as *The Wanderer* and *The Seafarer* explore the theme of exile and the desolation of losing a lord's friendship and protection:

> . . . long ago, the ground's shroud
> Enwrapped my gold friend. Wretched I went thence.
>
> (*The Wanderer*)

It is very easy to see the people in the past as somehow different from us, almost less human. Perhaps they did not feel pain and joy as we do. Through their poetry, the earliest English can speak across the centuries and the strength of emotion conveyed leaves the reader in little doubt that they are communicating with a human being who shares their full range of personal experience. Love stories are also found, but do not always have happy endings. Banishment from a husband causes great bitterness and suffering. An exiled wife compares her predicament to happier people:

> Some lovers in this world
> Live dear to each other, lie warm together
> At days beginning. . .
>
> (*The Wife's Complaint*)

The scop's main performances took place in the hall of the lord during the evening and at feasts. Being wealthy enough to support a professional enter-tainer probably enhanced the lord's prestige, but he might be expected to be able to perform with a harp himself and this helps to explain why these instru-ments are found in royal burials such as Sutton Hoo. The harp was also probably passed around, with each person taking a turn at entertaining the assembled company.

Being a guest at an important lord's hall must have been the height of excitement for an early Anglo-Saxon. As well as the entertainment and food, giving gifts was an important activity. Hrothgar, the lord who Beowulf goes to help, is the 'giver of rings'. Sometimes these rings are called arm rings, but these gifts do not show up clearly in the archaeological record. Finger and arm rings are relatively rare finds and occur with women. During the sixth century, rings are found in men's graves as an integral part of a sword hilt. Perhaps these represent the favour of a lord. Hrothgar's wife, Wealhtheow, serves the guests with a 'horn of bright mead'. Women are seldom mentioned in the hall. When they do appear they are usually of high status and are either giving gifts or serving mead. Their role in providing hospitality was an important one. However, whether women of lower status had any part to play at these gatherings, apart from serving, is unclear.

The whole experience of the hall with its gifts, food and entertainment served a serious purpose because it bonded the lord and his people together with ties of obligation, emphasising mutual dependence which was crucial in a turbulent society with no police force and no welfare state. Family and the favour of the lord were all a person could hope to call on for sustenance and protection. A warrior in particular would be expected to repay the hospitality by fighting for his patron if necessary. It was a great disgrace not to fulfil this duty. In the poem, we learn that at Beowulf's hour of need he is betrayed by all but one of his retainers. It is only realistic to think that such acts of cowardice and treachery took place in real life as well as in myths. More modest versions of the activities of the hall probably occurred at different levels of society.

The voice is a versatile instrument available to almost everyone at any time. Singing would have been an obvious way for people to entertain themselves and each other. Songs can have a more formal and ritual use, as suggested by the evidence of the scop. Music probably also formed part of a funeral. Dirges and laments are referred to in poetry, including those sung for Beowulf himself.

The thrill of the chase

Pastimes of a more physical nature were also pursued, at least by the wealthier. Horse riding could be undertaken for pleasure as well as for practical purposes. Horse gear or even burials of the whole animal occur up and down the country. Wanlip in Leicestershire produced a bridle bit while Lakenheath in Suffolk is perhaps the most famous horse burial, owing to the richness of the fittings. Similar objects from Easington, County Durham may also come from a highly embellished horse harness. Perhaps some believed that riding would form part of the afterlife.

65 *Scene showing a procession of deer from an urn of unknown origin. These animals were hunted.* Redrawn by R. Knox from Myres

Remains of deer from burial and settlement sites show that they were hunted. Although this has the practical outcome of providing extra food it has been enjoyed by the privileged for centuries as the ultimate sport, which helped keep them fit and ready for battle. Dogs may have been used to hunt. A cremation urn from Spong Hill is decorated with a scene showing a dog chasing a deer. Other pots with possible hunting motifs have been found at Caistor-by-Norwich (**65**). In late Anglo-Saxon times, woodland was specifically managed to improve hunting. Dogs were used to hunt wild boar as well as deer. Wolves, foxes, beaver, otters, hares and wildcats may also have fallen prey to the early English hunter (Hooke, D. 1998).

It is probable that birds were used for hunting, but there is little surviving evidence from the early period. Claws from a bird of prey were found in a cremation at Spong Hill. They were pierced so they could be worn, possibly as amulets. They may have been taken from a wild bird, but perhaps they came from a prized hunting bird after it had died. The use of hawks is mentioned in poems, including *Beowulf,* and the tenth-century *Battle of Maldon.* The peregrine falcon, sparrow hawk and goshawk are all native to Britain and later Anglo-Saxon sources state that young birds were taken from the wild in autumn and then trained. Any open land is suitable for hawking, but wetlands are particularly good because of the abundance of wildfowl (Hooke, D. 1998).

Children and toys

The evidence for early Anglo-Saxon toys is sparse. In cemeteries, children's graves often have no grave goods. Those that are furnished usually contain only a pot, a knife or a few beads. When children were buried with more possessions, they tended to be those associated with an adult. Many objects in graves are now fragmentary, having lost any organic components and can be hard to identify, so it is possible that at least a few of these may originally have been toys. At Chessell Down, one child's grave contained an incomplete object that may have been a rattle. Settlement sites do not tend to produce finds that can be recognised as toys. This does not mean that play and playthings were absent from childhood.

Toys are likely to have been made from scraps of organic materials such as cloth, wood and leather. These are relatively cheap, durable and safe with no sharp edges. Such resources could have been used to make balls, animals and dolls. Toys like these are known from Roman times and wall paintings also show children playing games like leap frog and blind man's buff. Children use their imagination, especially to emulate their superiors and heroes. In a period of settlement with its accompanying armed conflict, 'Angles and Britons' may have been an Anglo-Saxon version of 'Cowboys and Indians'.

Children will find things to play with whether they are given toys or not. Everybody knows that a child given an expensive present will still play with the wrapping paper and the box. Anglo-Saxon toddlers and children would have played with anything around them that was not moved out of reach. A wooden spoon can be a marvellous toy. It can be banged against other things to make a noise, it can be chewed or thrown repeatedly on the floor for the grown-ups to fetch. As a child grows older the spoon can become a doll with the addition of a cloth cape and a carved or painted face. Even in the nineteenth century, poorer families sometimes made dolls from legs of old chairs or tables.

Cats and dogs shared the farmstead with humans. Although they were kept to work, such as for vermin control and hunting, animals and children tend to form relationships. Dog burials occur in a number of cemeteries and a boy at Great Chesterford was accompanied by one.

Small children take great delight in 'helping' adults with daily tasks such as feeding animals or working in the garden. It is easy to envisage that what began as play would become a responsibility, as soon as the child was competent. Another reason why Anglo-Saxon childhood is hard to detect is because it was considerably shorter than in modern Britain.

7 The supernatural

From the human perspective, the world falls into two categories: things which they can influence such as planting seed, building homes and weaving cloth; and those which they cannot, including how much rain falls and gale force winds. The human brain, however, wants to rationalise even those things that it cannot control or understand. If explanations are not found in the natural world around them, people tend to look for supernatural answers. The supernatural world is complex and diverse with varying levels of power exercised by different forces. Gods and goddesses control the world, inexplicable events can be caused by monsters and other beings while some humans have access to superhuman abilities. All these entities prompt a response from the mere mortal. Deities are feared, worshipped and placated; powerful creatures must be avoided or kept at bay, and the wise or gifted person will be revered or persecuted depending on the situation.

The earliest English were faced with many situations they could not possibly understand. Disease and death were often close companions and a freak storm or other severe weather conditions could wreak havoc. A failed harvest or sick livestock could devastate a community. When the spear and shield could not provide adequate protection, other ways of surviving had to be found.

Finding out what they thought: problems and possibilities

Faith and superstition are perhaps two of the hardest areas of early Anglo-Saxon life to uncover. Information relating to these matters is fragmentary and disparate. In the Anglo-Saxon period, a spiritual conflict took place between pagan and Christian beliefs and eventually it was Christianity that displaced the pagan faiths. In any sort of conflict it is always better to be on the winning side. One advantage is that the victorious write the accounts of what happened and sometimes theirs is the only version that survives.

Christian monks brought writing with them and began to record not only current affairs but also the history of the land. However, they had no wish to preserve or treat objectively the religious practices which they believed had condemned their ancestors to the torments of hell. Some surviving Anglo-Saxon poetry probably originated in the oral tradition of the pagan period, but it is preserved in a written form, taken down in the Christian period. It seems likely that the now distasteful, pagan elements were edited out and some Christian passages were added in.

Place name studies have been used to identify areas with religious associations. Some, even today, preserve the name of a pagan god or goddess. This does not tell us why the place was special to that deity, nor what, if any, type of worship took place there.

Objects from graves and settlements can be scrutinised to see if they preserve any religious or superstitious meaning. However, this is highly problematic because it is not possible to get inside the mind of a person who lived 1,500 years ago. Today, we may look at an object and see symbols and meaning which are quite different from their Anglo-Saxon owner's. We may miss crucial symbols or attribute magical or spiritual significance to objects that had no such importance in the past. What follows is a tentative attempt to look at the evidence available and the possibilities it provides, rather than offering definitive answers.

Kept for protection

Some objects from Anglo-Saxon graves have an obvious practical purpose such as a buckle or a knife. Others are much more difficult to identify because only part of the object has survived, or they are so far removed from modern experience that no practical function can now be assigned to them. Attempting to understand these artefacts has led to the suggestion that some may be amulets.

Amulets are items specifically kept to protect the owner from harm, or to influence events in a positive manner. They can be materials that occur in nature, either vegetable or mineral, or can be manmade. Their power can come from their appearance, such as shape, colour or beauty. Potency can be associated with a natural property or attribute of the plant, stone or animal from which the amulet comes. Items may not start out as amulets but may be empowered and take on a new role, particularly if associated with a narrow escape from danger or a particularly good experience. This also means that an amulet can be very personal and impossible to recognise by someone not privy to its history. Vegetable amulets present specific problems because they are very unlikely to survive in the archaeological record. Many Anglo-Saxon artefacts have the properties of an amulet suggested for them, a very small selection of which is discussed below.

Teeth, tusks and claws are found in cemeteries up and down the country (**66**). They were usually pierced or mounted to allow them to be worn suspended, often in a necklace with beads. Canine teeth are relatively frequent finds, but it can be difficult to distinguish between wolf and dog's teeth. At first glance this might seem like an appropriate amulet for a warrior, imbuing the wearer with the ferocity and the cunning of a wild hunter. However,

66 *Pierced tusk from Lechlade, possibly worn as an amulet or charm (9.5cm long).* Redrawn by R. Knox from Boyle, Jennings and Miles

pierced teeth are usually found with adult women. Boars are another fierce creature that would be appropriate for a warrior to wish to draw strength from, but boars' tusks also tend to accompany women or children. At Lechlade, a tusk was buried with a 12-year-old child, the only other item in the grave being a buckle. Boars are also known for their fertility and it could be this attribute that tusk amulets are drawing on, to ensure the owner could have children or to protect them through pregnancy. However, the young person from Lechlade, if female, would only just be able to bear children, if she had reached puberty at all. A mature or older adult from Spong Hill was found with a tusk. Unless she was infertile, it is likely that she had already had several children and may even have been through the menopause. If tusks were an amulet to ensure and protect fertility it seems that they could be significant both before and after childbearing age. It is not known whether they were sometimes passed on rather than being buried with the deceased, but it is possible that their power was restricted to one individual and so they stayed with that person even after death. More examples from cemeteries with sexed and aged skeletons may help to clarify the matter in the future.

Beaver tooth pendants are known from a small number of sites. They most often occur in the graves of moderately wealthy women. A woman from West Heslerton had grave goods including annular brooches, a silver bead, silver ring, and girdle hangers as well as a type of amulet. Beavers were still living in the wild during Anglo-Saxon times and the strength of their teeth must have been both obvious and impressive. Anything that can chew through a tree would make short work of an Anglo-Saxon loaf, no matter how coarse and gritty. This has prompted the suggestion that their teeth, and perhaps all tooth pendants, were thought to protect the wearer from dental decay and disease. This sounds perfectly logical but does not explain why their use was restricted to women. Early English men suffered from dental problems as much as the women. Beavers use the wood they bring down to build dams and lodges as homes. Perhaps a beaver tooth amulet may be associated with providing for the physical needs of the family: shelter, warmth and food. This is likely to have been the woman's sphere of responsibility and perhaps such an amulet was to protect and empower the custodian of the home. A man buried at Lechlade was accompanied by the whole skeleton of a rook or crow. It is possible that this had a supernatural motive but a precise meaning is elusive.

Cowrie shells are found in a number of graves (**67**). A small example, probably collected from a nearby beach, was found at Norton. Most cowries were exotic imports from the Indian Ocean and occur with relatively wealthy women. One lady from Lechlade was buried with fragments of silver and 200 small garnets as well as a cowrie. These shells often seem to have been buried in a bag or box, sometimes by the feet as in a grave at Buckland, or between the legs, as at Kingston Down. Such bags and boxes often contain other items that are thought to have the properties of an amulet. However, the use of boxes may reflect a move away from carrying precious objects with the individual. Most graves containing cowries date to the seventh century, when the practice of burying things with people was coming to an end. Fashions in costume were also changing significantly, with brooches and other dress fastenings no longer being such an integral part of garments. It was also a time when Christian missionaries were spreading the new faith and converting many Anglo-Saxons. If cowrie shells were being used as amulets at this late date it could indicate that the people may have been willing to accept new beliefs but were not necessarily going to let go of superstitions.

Cowrie shells are often interpreted as fertility amulets because their shape mirrors female genitalia. This intimate symbol may be reflected by keeping the shell out of sight, rather than wearing it openly. However, they were buried with children including a nine-year-old from Lechlade who had four

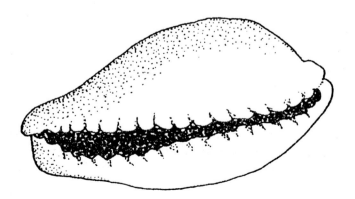

67 *Cowrie shells were usually exotic imports that may have been treasured for supernatural powers (6cm long).* Drawn by R. Knox

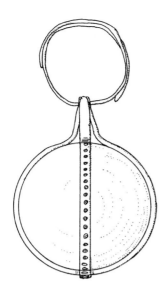

68 *Balls of rock crystal, perhaps thought to be magical, are found with some wealthy women in Kent and the Isle of Wight.* Redrawn by R. Knox from Arnold

as well as silver sheet fragments, sliver wire necklace rings and a bucket fitting. Therefore, any enhancement or protection of fertility could include that expected for the future.

There are other possible explanations. This shell also resembles an eye. Excavations at Jericho discovered skulls with plaster moulded over them to create a model of a face. Cowrie shells were set into the eye sockets. If the Anglo-Saxons saw a similarity between these shells and human eyes, as the people of Jericho did, then they could have been prized for protecting sight. Other types of shells including cockle, limpet and mussel are found in graves, although not often. These too may have had supernatural powers, but could equally have been included as food.

A mineral, which is often ascribed as having special properties, is rock crystal. Small crystal beads, which are colourless and transparent like modern glass, are found relatively frequently on necklaces. However, crystal was used in two more dramatic and ostentatious ways; as crystal balls and as large, perforated pieces shaped with many facets, in a similar manner to modern gemstones. Crystal was probably another expensive import (Meaney, A. 1981).

Crystal balls are usually around 45mm in diameter and suspended in a metal sling (**68**). This was sometimes a precious metal such as the silver example from Chessell Down, emphasising the value of these items. Crystal balls are not common. They date from the fifth to the seventh centuries and finds concentrate around Kent and the Isle of Wight, the areas traditionally linked with Jutish settlers. Once more they accompany women who were given rich burials. At Chessell Down, one grave included a bronze bucket decorated with a hunting scene; five brooches, one of silver with inlaid garnets; fragments of gold braid; an iron weaving batten; gold and silver finger rings as well as a perforated silver spoon and a ball made of smoky crystal. Spoons with numerous holes through their bowls are repeatedly found in conjunction with crystal balls, which implies they formed some sort of set. It has been proposed that they could be used for removing sediment from wine or finings from beer. Alternatively, the crystal may have been used to concentrate the sun's rays and start fires, but the role of the spoon in this case is obscure. Such properties may have had a magical or spiritual significance to the Anglo-Saxons. Even if the crystal ball was a practical object it could still be regarded as an amulet, protecting the supply of drink or the hearth of a home, which was crucial for both heating and cooking. But there are further complications. These are elegant objects of some beauty. If they were amulets, they were the preserve of the rich in a restricted geographical area. It is possible that they were not supernatural objects of protection at all but imported status symbols, the preserve of the upper strata of one section of Anglo-Saxon society.

A curious discovery from a different region of the country seems to mimic the suspended crystal ball. At West Heslerton, in two separate graves, walnuts were discovered in metal cradles with triangular metal spangles hanging beneath. Both graves were of young women and dated to the last half of the sixth century. It is not certain when walnuts were introduced to this country so these examples could be imports. How or what these objects were meant to protect or encourage is a mystery. Nuts would be an important food source, especially because they keep for such long periods. The resemblance of a walnut to the human brain with the shell as the skull springs to mind, but this is purely guesswork.

Faceted crystals have a much wider geographical range but were still a luxury item (**colour plate 25**). Their shape, size and number of facets vary and so did their function. Some, even the very large, are found with necklaces and appear to have been used as huge beads. Others are found singly near the thighs, as at Glen Parva, Leicestershire, and appear to have been spindle whorls, a weight used in spinning. The facets would cause the crystal to sparkle and may even have refracted daylight to produce rainbow colours (Meaney, A. 1981), particularly if the lady of the house was standing in the sunshine, chatting and spinning with other women, using their own utilitarian and dowdy spindles with whorls made of bone or clay. The effect of the crystal would be beautiful and quite possibly magical. This would concentrate visual attention on the object that would in turn make it the perfect amulet for attracting the 'Evil Eye' away from the owner. This malevolence could be the malicious envy or intention of another person or creature. Where it is possible to tell, faceted crystals are found with adult women, the section of the community who bore children and cared for the home. Perhaps evil creatures were jealous of family bonds and mutual support. Crystals, therefore, particularly as spindle whorls, may have been used to protect the leading women within a kinship group, recognising the importance of their roles as spinner and weaver, the one who provides clothes and blankets to protect her people from the cold.

A potential category of amulet, which falls between animal and mineral, are fossils (the remains of prehistoric creatures which have been turned to stone). Porosphaera are small fossil sponges with naturally occurring holes. These are occasionally found as a part of bead strings. They may have been collected out of Anglo-Saxon practicality: why waste a ready-made bead? However, supernatural significance cannot be ruled out, particularly because one was found with a horse burial at Great Chesterford.

Fossil sea urchins (echinoids) seem a stronger contender for supernatural status. These tend to have lost their spines, but the shell that remains is roughly spherical or heart shaped. At Westgarth Gardens, an echinoid was found in the right hand of an adult woman who was buried with brooches, beads and wrist clasps. At Buckland, one was buried, probably in a box, with a child under seven years of age. This burial was dated to around AD 625 to 650. The shape and size of a fossil sea urchin resembles a bread roll which has led to the suggestion that these were used as amulets to ensure that the owner never went hungry. This would make it an appropriate object of protection for both adults and children. If the harvest failed, the whole community suffered. Hunger was often accompanied by sickness, and echinoids may have been attributed with the power to heal. A young woman from Edix Hill, who may have had leprosy, was perhaps hoping that her fossil would alleviate her suffering. In more recent times, echinoids were thought to be made by lightning striking the earth and were kept to ward off storms, the reasoning being that lightning never strikes the same place twice. The same explanation has also been used for fossil belemnites, Neolithic polished stone axes and rock crystals. Even today, with a vastly increased population, a person is very unlikely to be struck by lightning. This begs the question, were people in the past so anxious about such an unlikely event? There were many more equally nasty occurrences, which were far more likely to happen. Perhaps this fear embodies a serious dread of the devastation that can be caused to crops and buildings by storms. In exceptional circumstances, livestock can be electrocuted by lightning striking waterlogged ground.

A belemnite was found with a young woman at Beckford. As well as thunderstones, belemnites (which tend to be long and pointy) were thought to be elf shot, arrows that might have been loosed at people or animals. Carrying one would be protection against a future attack.

Finally, amulets can be manmade. Roman coins are frequently found in both cremation and inhumation graves, but they were not being used as money. Coins usually have a face on one side and so the wearer would literally have someone else looking out for them and this has led to the suggestion that they may have been kept for superstitious reasons. Many were deliberately pierced so they could be worn and were often included in bead strings.

Where it is possible to identify the sex of an individual, pierced coins are found with women. They were buried with babies, children, adolescents, adults and older people and the practice was followed from the north to the south of England. The coin may be the only artefact found in the grave, as with some of the cremations at Spong Hill, or it may be one of many finds such as the 45-year-old lady from Andover who was buried with three brooches, a pin, comb, knife, buckle and beads.

Coins that were not perforated have also been discovered with infants, young people and adults in inhumations and cremations. Sometimes they were situated near the legs or waist and could have been in a bag or pouch. Occasionally, they are found with men and at Great Chesterford one accompanied a dog.

Unlike other possible amulets, coins seem to have been available to practically anyone who wanted to take advantage of them, including relatives trying to protect their dead baby. Perhaps their extensive use reflects the faith of the earliest English in the power of the face and furthermore, it is a motif incorporated into designs on a number of their brooch types. Alternatively, their use may illustrate the ease with which it was possible to acquire them. Roman coins appear to have been used as gaming pieces so they were not necessarily treated as sacred items, reserved for special use. However, there remains the possibility that the Anglo-Saxons thought it appropriate to use them for both purposes. The practice of wearing coins was very long lived. When the Anglo-Saxons introduced them as currency, some were still converted into pendants and worn, including a coin dating to about AD 670 from Lechlade.

Who used amulets?

The few examples above serve to demonstrate the range of material that today is interpreted as having magical meaning to the early Anglo-Saxons. Caution is needed when viewing objects in this way. Some items, like rock crystal balls and cowrie shells, were rare imports, controlled by the wealthy. Therefore, their importance may have been in signifying a person's position in society rather than providing protection. The height of their use coincides with the period of conversion to Christianity, which suggests that even if some spiritual beliefs changed, superstition did not decrease.

Fossils may have been regarded as having unearthly powers, but could have been curiosities. Pierced Roman coins were well distributed both socially and geographically, and this may be evidence for a strong and widespread conviction of their potency, but again this is not certain. Many Roman and prehistoric objects are found deliberately buried with Anglo-Saxon people, from Roman pots and brooches to Iron Age beads and chariot fittings. All of these may have a sacred property or, as the poem *Beowulf* suggests, the folk of this time were attracted to relics of the past, so much so that they could be used as gifts to settle feuds:

> sent to the Wylfings over the water's back
> Old things of beauty. . .
>
> (*Beowulf*)

Very few objects are found with men and it is hard to identify ones that may have been considered as amulets. Rings and beads associated with swords may fall into this category but are rare. Sword beads may also have had a practical function, helping to fasten the scabbard onto a sword belt or tying the sword into the scabbard. There are a number of possible explanations for the lack of evidence of superstition among men. It may be that amulets appropriate for men differed from women's. If they were made of organic materials, such as wood or plant matter, they simply would not survive in an inhumation grave or would be immediately consumed by fire in a cremation. Men may have used protective objects in life but, for reasons that are lost to us, it was forbidden or unnecessary for men to retain them after death. Women and children could have been perceived as the ones who were most vulnerable, needing extra protection. There is support for this when taking into account the fact that about one in four children died before adulthood, whilst women had a shorter life expectancy than men. However, men may have amulets in their graves, which are not recognised as such today. The predominant type of object found in male graves is weaponry, including spears, swords and shields. Although these were practical, used in physical combat, they may have served the same purposes on a supernatural level.

All the potential amulet types discussed above have one thing in common: they were all found with the dead. If these objects were supposed to give protection and ensure a favourable outcome, it could be argued that they had failed, especially those accompanying children. If the items had a specific purpose, such as a boar's tusk worn for fertility, they may have achieved their purpose during the person's life. Why were they not passed on so that another could benefit from their power, and why were unsuccessful magical artefacts deemed worthy of inclusion in the grave? It may be that such objects were magically bound to an individual and would not work for anyone else, or it is conceivable that they were needed in an afterlife. In other instances, amulets might have been passed on several times before finally being deposited in a grave, but there is now no way to tell.

Despite all of the potential pitfalls when assigning magical powers to objects, it is likely that the early Anglo-Saxons were very superstitious. There was much around them they could not hope to understand and there were many things to fear. Today we know much more about the universe around us and often understand why things happen even if they are beyond our control. This does not prevent us from trying to alter events using supernatural powers: lucky numbers for the lottery; a special pen for an exam or a treasured four-leaf clover, to mention but a few. Superstitions will be respected even when people do not believe in them. Fishermen's wives used to avoid hanging out washing on the day their husbands sailed for fear of calling up a wind. As the writer heard one say, they did not really believe this could happen, but they would not take the chance. People are not machines and even in a modern society they need more than logic.

Gods and goddesses

The early Anglo-Saxon deities share their origins with those of the Vikings. Pagan written sources do survive from Scandinavia but are of a later date. Stories, roles and even gods changed over time and the surviving written material has diverged from the beliefs of the pagan Anglo-Saxons. For example, it has been suggested that Balder, who was an important god in Scandinavian beliefs, was only a hero to the Anglo-Saxons, and the earliest English did not regard the pantheon as a family. However, comparison with Norse mythology can give an insight into the possible characters of Anglo-Saxon gods. Taking this into account, what can be pieced together about the spiritual side of Anglo-Saxon life?

Woden was one of the most important gods. He is the equivalent of the more Germanic Wotan and the later Viking, Odin. Woden's name is recorded in a number of English place names including Wednesfield in Staffordshire; Wensley meaning Woden's Wood in Derbyshire and Wormshill meaning

69 *Headdresses from a figure on the Sutton Hoo helmet and a pin from Buckland may be connected with Woden.* Drawn by R. Knox

Woden's Hill in Kent (Crocker, G. 1981). Wiltshire's Vale of Pewsey has a cluster of Woden related place names, perhaps indicating that he was particularly venerated there (Hutton, R. 1991). Woden often appeared to mortals in disguise and earned the nickname Grim. Grimsburyburg in Oxfordshire may, therefore, also be a reference to him. By the tenth century, his character was firmly linked with cunning and deceit. As well as places, his name is preserved in the day of the week, Wednesday.

Woden traditionally created disagreement between the gods by throwing a spear among them and so this weapon is associated with him. A buckle from Finglesham, Kent probably shows Woden or one of his followers. It is decorated with a man who holds a spear in each hand and is naked apart from a belt and buckle. He wears a strange headdress or helmet with protruding horns, which terminate in eagles' heads meeting face-to-face. Very similar headgear is seen on two warriors in a panel on the helmet from the kingly ship burial at Sutton Hoo. The men carry spears but also swords and seem to be engaged in a ritual dance. Perhaps this illustrates a component of the worship of Woden. A pin from Buckland bears the same eagle helmet motif. No bones survived in the grave, but other grave goods, including beads, suggest this was probably a woman who was buried between AD 675 and 700 (**69**). The dating is crucial because it is well into the period of Christian conversions and implies that some sections of the population were not only holding on to pagan beliefs, but were at pains to visibly demonstrate their faith.

Two wolves and two ravens were Woden's familiars and they kept him informed about what was said and done, both by the living and the dead. The purse mount from Sutton Hoo shows a man, possibly the god, flanked by two wolves who either seem to be devouring him or whispering into his ears (**70**). Woden was also associated with human sacrifice by hanging. He was hanged for nine days on a tree, pierced by a spear and so learnt wisdom and the secret of runes, Anglo-Saxon letters. There is a possibility that this is a later, Scandinavian belief. However, the medical text the *Lacnunga*, mentions Woden in what has become known as the Nine Herb Charm. The god kills an adder using nine glory rods and it has been argued that these were made of wood, marked with runes. The serpent flies into nine parts creating nine cures to nine poisons and maladies in the form of herbs. This text was written down in the Christian period and the fact that reference to a pagan deity survives indicates his persisting importance.

Woden was also the leader of the 'savage hunt' or the 'furious army'. The legend goes that on certain stormy nights, the ghosts of dead warriors can be heard as they gallop across the skies. He is sometimes represented on horseback as a reference to this myth. Presumably, this contributes to later folklore about 'Herne the Hunter' and the 'Wild Hunt'. Anglo-Saxon society was based on the warrior class and military endeavour that is reflected back onto their gods. Woden presided over the hall where chosen dead warriors spent their time feasting and in martial pastimes. The most common types of

70 *This figure from the Sutton Hoo helmet is either being devoured by wolves or it is Woden listening to news from his familiars.* Drawn by R. Knox

artefact found with early English men are weapons and feasting equipment that suggests they were probably hoping to spend the afterlife revelling in Woden's Hall.

Woden used magic to rule and had an interest in the Other World, not just the world of people. He was a god who did not fight in battle, but might use magic to intervene. Sometimes he would cause paralysing panic. However, he could be called upon to cure sprains and dislocations.

Hengist and Horsa, the traditional leaders of the first settlers, claimed to be descended from Woden. Bede records that before they set out for Britain the brothers invoked him to gain his assistance. Six out of eight Anglo-Saxon royal houses included Woden in their ancestry. Some, including Wessex and Kent, did not include him originally, but he was significant enough to be added. Woden was perhaps revered more by the royal households than people of lower status because he was their godly equivalent.

Thunor, or the more Germanic Donar, is another important god but of a lower station than Woden in most areas. The Vikings knew him as Thor, Odin's son. A number of place names show he was recognised in England, such as Thundersley in Essex, Thunderfield in Surrey and Thunerleaw in Kent. Thunreslau in Essex associates him with a pillar that may have been used in his worship, perhaps representing a sacred tree. Thunor is remembered in the day of the week, Thursday, Donar in the German Donnerstag.

Thunor was a god of thunder, made by the wheels of his chariot travelling across the heavens and even the word derives from his name. Some considered him the most powerful of the gods and he was greatly feared. He was also a god of war and his weapon was a stone hammer or a throwing axe. Pendants worn for protection or luck showing the hammer (Thor's hammer) were not worn until the Viking raids and settlements during Christian Anglo-Saxon times. The swastika symbol was also associated with Thunor, but did not have the same sinister connotations as it does today. The arms of the swastika may represent lightning. Circular brooches were made using the swastika with open-work cut between the lightening forks (**71**). The shape of these holes is very similar to an Anglo-Saxon hammer, so the brooches may be incorporating two of Thunor's symbols in one. These brooches are particularly common in the Midlands and Yorkshire. As would be expected of brooches, they are found with women, predominantly adults, but on rare occasions they are found with children, including a three-year-old from Broughton Lodge. A square-headed brooch from the same site was decorated with a swastika motif, and also comes from a young child's burial.

Swastika patterns were used on some cremation urns, from areas traditionally associated with Anglian settlers. In some cases, the emblem was carved onto a stamp and impressed into the soft clay before firing. Swastikas could be made of additional pieces of clay and applied to the pot's surface creating a raised effect (**72**). On other urns, the design was drawn freehand as an integral part of the decoration scheme but occasionally it seems to have been added afterwards. This implies that the swastika did have a particular significance and needed to be on the vessel, even if it was a later addition. It also

71 *The swastika was incorporated into a type of open-work brooch like this one from Empingham.* Photograph by A. Kemp, courtesy of Anglian Water

suggests that cinerary urns were not necessarily made to order specifically for the individual or it would have been possible to ensure the motif was incorporated from the outset. Infants, children and adults of both sexes were interred in urns bearing swastikas. If this shows an allegiance to the god Thunor, then it was a widespread and popular faith, particularly in the Midlands and the North and East Anglia, but the emblem is also found on a sixth-century sword from Bifrons and a seventh-century cloisonné brooch from Faversham in Kent. It appears to have been an inclusive religion, open to men and women of all ages. Urns decorated with the design may contain no grave goods or many, indicating that wealth or the lack of it, did not exclude an individual from following Thunor.

Tiw or Tyr was another god whose name is preserved in place-names including Tyresmere in Worcester and Tysoe in Warwickshire. Tiw is the origin of Tuesday. Tiw was originally the patron of the legal side of government but became more associated with rules governing battle. He is often represented by a spear, which was a sign of judicial power as well as a weapon. Tiw's name is also represented by a rune: ↑. This rune has been found on a sword from Faversham, a spear from Holborough and possibly a sword pommel from Gilton in Kent. Tiw's rune also appears on cremation urns, but not nearly as frequently as the swastika. It was stamped onto pots from

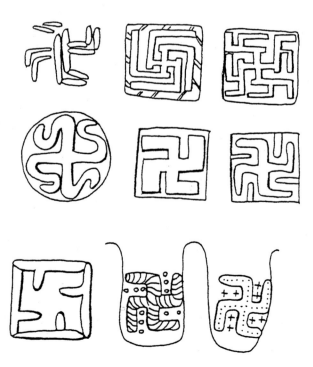

72 *Swastika designs, in many forms, were used on cremation urns.* Drawn by R. Knox

Kettering in Northamptonshire, Lackford in Suffolk and Girton in Cambridgeshire. In other cases it was drawn freehand or added in relief. However, it is not always possible to be certain whether this was a deliberate representation of the rune or just a chevron design incorporating vertical lines at intervals. Possible examples are geographically widespread from Yorkshire to East Anglia and as far south as the Isle of Wight.

Ing was another god represented by his own rune. He was a fertility deity but little else is known of him. It is thought that Ing may be another name for the better-known Freyr. The name Freyr has not yet been found in England, but in Scandinavia he is a god of fertility. Both he and his twin sister, Freyja, were associated with boars and Freyr's chariot was pulled by a boar with golden bristles. Boar crests have been found on both the Benty Grange and Pioneer helmets, from Derbyshire and Northamptonshire respectively. Helmets are very rare finds from the early Anglo-Saxon period and the occurrence of the boar crest with two emphasises their significance and supports the frequent mentions of such helmets in *Beowulf*. The hero himself is given a standard decorated with the animal. Boars form part of the decoration of the gold and garnet clasps from the boat burial at Sutton Hoo. Bearing in mind the ferocity and courage of the wild boar, it is not surprising that a warrior would want to take on the characteristics. As discussed above, boar tusks are found which have been made into pendants worn by women, perhaps representing the woman as protector of the home or reflecting on the fertility of the animal. Boar's tusks do not always occur with an individual and at Butt Close Lane in Leicester one was found in an Anglo-Saxon well (**73**). It was part of an interesting group of objects including a Neolithic (New Stone Age) polished stone axe, a pierced tooth and Anglo-Saxon bone ring. Throwing objects into water such as springs, lakes and rivers has been practised during many times in the past and survives today when people toss coins into fountains and wishing wells. It seems likely that the Butt Close Lane assemblage has a supernatural motive and was possibly an offering to Freyr or Freyja.

Freyr's name is related to the Anglo-Saxon word meaning 'lord' which was adopted by the Christians to be used for God. Freyr, the young and handsome god, may have been connected in peoples' minds with Christ, the God who chose to die in his prime to save mankind.

Loki was a mischief-maker and worked to undermine the power of the other gods. In Scandinavian mythology, it is Loki who finally brings about the destruction of the gods. It has been suggested that Loki may be a later addition to the Norse gods and was not known to the pagan Anglo-Saxons.

Friga or Frigg was the wife of Woden. Fridaythorpe in Yorkshire, Frobury in Hampshire and Fretherne in Gloucestershire all preserve her name. Friday is named after her. She was the goddess of childbirth and marriage. Frigg was sometimes attributed with foreknowledge. Kathleen Herbert suggests Freo may be a more linguistically appropriate translation of her name.

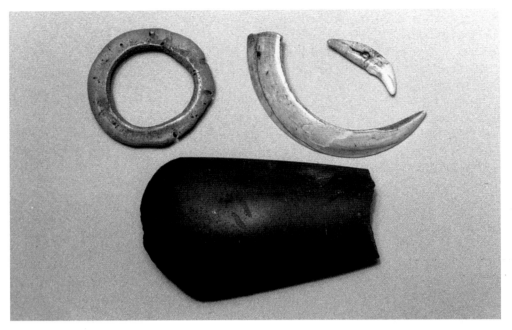

73 *Group of objects, possibly with religious or supernatural connections, from a well in Leicester.* Photograph by A. Kemp, courtesy of Jewry Wall Museum, Leicester

Freyja is often confused with Freo and is sometimes referred to as the wife of Woden. There is such a great overlap between Freyja and Freo that they can become almost indistinguishable. Freyja is said to have had a great hall in the sky for receiving dead warriors of whom she had the pick. She was the first of the Valkyries and their supreme commander. She was also fond of jewellery and once slept with four dwarves for a particularly fine necklace.

Other goddesses are known in less detail. March, the last month of winter, was called Rheda's month by the earliest English and Bede says that sacrifices were made to her then. Her name is associated with the words for 'glory, fame, triumph', but also 'fierce, cruel' and Herbert has suggested that Rheda is connected with the waelcyries, the Anglo-Saxon version of the Valkyries, who take the souls of fallen warriors from the battlefield (Herbert, K. 1994). Eostre was a goddess of dawn, rebirth and fertility. She was associated with spring and her name gave rise to the word Easter. April was known as Eostre's month and it is likely that a specific festival or act of worship took place in her honour at this time of year. Sif was the wife of Thunor. The names that do survive probably represent the minimum number of divine beings. It is possible that others have survived only in place names and cannot now be recognised.

Bede records the names of other months and alludes to their pagan religious significance, but as a Christian monk he does not to go into detail. September was Holy Month when tribute was paid to the gods. This would coincide with the end of harvest, as Harvest Festival does in the Christian Church today, and so it seems most plausible that offerings of produce were made. However, today in the north, Harvest Festivals tend to be celebrated a couple of weeks after those in the Midlands because of the later harvest so it is possible that precise dates for ceremonies depended on the circumstances of the region. November was blood month when sacrifices were made. This is another festival with a practical aspect because this is the time of year when animals not being kept over winter would be slaughtered and meat was relatively abundant. Thanks would be given, probably associated with feasting before the more frugal rationing of winter and spring. When making offerings to the divine, it is best to do it in circumstances when the people do not have to go without themselves, although the gods may not see it like that. Midwinter saw one of the most important celebrations, Mothers' Night. However, Bede does not record who the Mothers were or what took place. Mother earth has been venerated by many peoples in many places so this may be a manifestation of the same deity. The Roman historian Tacitus records that an earth mother goddess was worshipped in the Germanic homelands around the first century AD. Here she was known as Nerthus and lived in a shrine but once a year would journey through the land on a sacred cart accompanied by a male consort. At the end of the progress the cart was washed but the animals and the male companion were drowned. Whether some version of this crossed to England with the settlers is feasible but uncertain.

Anglo-Saxon places of worship are even more elusive. No obvious shrines or temples survive, not least because of the early Anglo-Saxon tradition of building in wood and not stone. Christian missionaries were advised to convert pagan buildings into churches to help people change their faith more easily and so any surviving remains could be buried underneath churches. Excavations at the royal site of Yeavering in Northumberland have produced evidence of structures with possible religious significance including one, which may have acted like an amphitheatre, enabling a person or small group to address a large audience. Ironically, such evidence as survives was preserved by Bede who mentions pagan shrines a number of times in his account of the conversion of the Anglo-Saxons to Christianity: Raedwald of East Anglia hedged his bets by setting up a Christian altar in his temple next to a pagan one. In Northumbria, a pagan temple was desecrated by throwing a spear into it and during a plague in AD 665 the East Saxons began to rebuild ruined pagan temples. However, 'ealh' meaning temple is found in very few places, and those which survive are in Kent.

There is evidence that physical representations of the gods were made, idols are referred to when King Sigbert of the East Saxons is finally persuaded that objects made by man from wood and stone cannot be gods. The account of the conversion of King Edwin of Northumbria provides extra details that deities were served by priests who were not allowed to carry weapons or ride stallions. Taking all the snippets together, there was some type of formal religion, closely associated with the royal families. Holy buildings housed altars to gods where sacrifices were made. In *Beowulf*, people pray and make vows at altars when asking to be delivered from the monster, Grendel. Priests probably officiated at ceremonies or at least cared for the temples. These men (no reference survives to priestesses) were set apart from other important males because they were removed from the warrior, weapon-bearing class.

Other centres of worship are attested in place names. 'Hill top sanctuary' denoted by the Anglo-Saxon 'hearh' occurs in the Midlands and south-east while 'woeh', a 'sacred space' is relatively common and 'leah' is a cleared space possibly associated with Woden or Thunor (Hutton, R. 1991). These convey that gods and goddesses were worshiped outside in natural or altered environments as well as manmade structures.

Perhaps the most powerful supernatural force was 'wyrd'. This roughly equates to fate or destiny. The belief in this concept has left no definitely identifiable mark on the archaeological record but is referred to in later documents. Wyrd was often seen as destructive but it was also unchangeable and irresistible.

Creatures and monsters

A range of mythical creatures shared the existences of the earliest English and many were far from friendly. The most famous is perhaps the monster Grendel, Beowulf's vicious adversary. This creature hated humans and terrorised Hrothgar's Hall, killing and carrying off the elite of his war band. The dead warriors were eaten, one being consumed with sickening relish as Grendel:

> gnashed at his bone joints, bolted huge gobbets,
> sucked at his veins, and had soon eaten
> all of the dead man, down to his
> hands and feet. . .

The ogre attacked at night and lived in a lair in the marshlands by day. Grendel used magic and was protected by a spell that prevented blades from cutting into him. However, Beowulf was no ordinary warrior and managed to tear off the monster's arm, which proved a fatal wound. Even monsters have feelings and Grendel's mother is distraught at the death of her son. She takes bloody revenge on the warriors, but is pursued by Beowulf and killed.

The terror encountered by the hero late in his life was a dragon. Serpents, wyrms and dragons are similar types of creature in Anglo-Saxon folklore. Beowulf's assailant guards a hoard of treasure under a barrow until disturbed by a thief. As revenge, it uses its fiery breath to lay waste to the surrounding countryside, 'So the visitant began to vomit flames'. Sea serpents are also

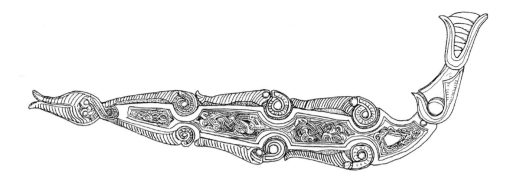

74 *A dragon, with particularly fierce teeth, from Sutton Hoo.* Drawn by R. Knox

mentioned in *Beowulf*. One of the artefacts from the Sutton Hoo ship burial is in the form of a dragon, with huge, vicious teeth (**74**). Many other objects are decorated with animal motifs (**75**). In the seventh century, creatures often have thin, elongated bodies that interlace with themselves and with their own limbs. Although it is not always easy to identify what the animal is, the sinuous style is very evocative of the wyrm or dragon.

Anglo-Saxon giants were of great size. They are mentioned as the builders of large stone structures such as in the poem *The Ruin*. In Norse mythology, the first living creature was a giant. Although not necessarily evil, both Odin and Thor have reason to fight with giants, but it is not certain that their Anglo-Saxon counterparts had similar relationships with such beings.

Elves originally encompassed a wide range of nature spirits. There were different kinds of elf and they lived in places such as hills, forests, moors and by water including the sea. Elves were archers and were not averse to shooting

75 *A less intimidating wyrm from an urn.* Redrawn by R. Knox from Myre

149

animals and people. Several cures in the *Lacnunga* are for countering elf shot, probably in reality sudden, shooting pains with no apparent cause, such as stitch. They could also be responsible for nightmares. However, elves were considered to be beautiful and it was a great compliment to refer to a lady as elf fair. They also had wisdom and secret knowledge. 'Aelf' meaning 'elf' appears in many Anglo-Saxon names including Aelfred.

Dwarves lived underground and were usually bearded, often hunchbacked or ugly. However, they were extremely skilled. Norse mythology records that they made Odin's spear and Thor's hammer, which were weapons so powerful that they could not be deflected once aimed at a target. Dwarves also fabricated jewellery for goddesses. Like elves, they were not necessarily friendly to humans and the *Lacnunga* includes charms to protect people from them. The illness associated with dwarves tends to be a fever.

Finally, there were people who had access to special skills and knowledge. Some of the remedies in the *Lacnunga* are for maladies caused by witches. Belief in magic, both good, in the form of amulets, and bad, seems to have been embedded in society. Another legendary figure illustrates the crossover between a practical skill and a supernatural power. The story of Weland (Wayland) the Smith can be pieced together from a number of sources. The poem *Deor* tells how Nithhad hamstrings Weland, presumably because he was such a good metalworker and Nithhad intends to prevent him from leaving. In revenge, the smith murders Nithhad's sons, rapes his daughter and makes her pregnant. A whalebone casket dating to the eighth century shows Weland at his forge, making cups from the dead men's skulls. The bodies can be seen under his feet and the young woman stands before him. Weland's skill is attested in other poems. Beowulf has a mail shirt made by him and the hero Waldere a sword. Turning metal into formidable weapons or armour must have seemed like a magical act. The flames and heat of the forge must have added to a sense of the unnatural. If smiths were itinerant, their skills would be seen less often by most people which would add to the feeling that their work required supernatural powers to transform the materials.

The review above only serves to touch on the supernatural elements of Anglo-Saxon life. In many cases, specific details and meanings have been lost to us. However, coping with the things they could not physically control by using magic and invoking the help of the gods must have been an all-pervasive aspect of early English life.

8 Our fragile past

There is so much still to learn about the earliest English that every new find can be important. This is true for all the peoples who have gone before us and explains why there are measures in place which give some protection to our past.

Why preserve the past?

Collecting archaeological material and preserving it is a complex and expensive process. It is also a commitment for generations to come. If our society is to continue to make this investment then there must be reasons to justify it. How can archaeology compete for finances and support against, for example, healthcare and law and order? The simple answer is that it cannot. The National Health Service is essential for saving and enhancing life and without a police force no individual would ever be safe. These are necessities on which we all depend. However, when the institutions society needs to survive have been put in place, there then follows a whole range of opportunities that actually make life worth living. Archaeology is not essential for our survival but its potential to contribute to our quality of life is enormous.

Only by studying the past can people understand the society they live in. We are the heirs to all of those in this country that came before us, whether or not they were our biological ancestors. The decisions they made and actions they took affect how we live today. This book has tried to look at the lives of the earliest English, peoples who invaded and settled this land, as many had done before and as many have done since. Theirs was a multicultural society. Yet, in the early twenty-first century, we are so ignorant of this that an MP can complain of asylum seekers diluting the Anglo-Saxon gene pool. If we could come to terms with the fact that the English people in particular are the product of invaders, settlers, slaves and traders from throughout the world since the earliest humans walked here, then perhaps we could learn to understand and celebrate our rich and wonderful culture rather than seeing our diverse origins as barriers.

On a lighter level the past can be our playground. The Anglo-Saxon period was a dramatic time of conflict, change and struggle. We might not care to admit it but warfare and battles are fascinating, exciting subjects especially when the events cannot harm us or our loved ones. It was an epic time, the reality behind the legends of heroes, including King Arthur.

The objects left by our predecessors can stun us with their beauty, fascinate us with their ingenuity or perplex us with their strangeness. We have inherited many sources of delight and inspiration. There is still much to discover about the peoples who lived here in past times. The exploration can be the most absorbing and satisfying activity of all and can be undertaken on many levels.

Join the exploration

The most effective way of protecting our past is to preserve museums, excavation units and other archaeological organisations. In order to achieve this, those who fund such agencies must be convinced that they are needed and valued. The best way to achieve this is for as many people as possible to be involved in archaeology. There are various ways this can be done, with something to suit every age and circumstance.

Museums are required to provide statistics to show how well they are performing. Visitors are counted, so every individual making a trip to a museum is also giving their support in a very important way. Museums are particularly keen to encourage repeat visits and so, as well as permanent displays, they will try to stage temporary exhibitions. Family days and holiday clubs attempt to present archaeology in a more dynamic way. Everybody needs friends and museums are no exception. Friends' organisations often have a programme of previews to exhibitions, excursions and lectures. Some help out as volunteers, working on projects in the museum. Fund-raising is often an important role taken on by the Friends and with the increasing financial pressures exerted on museums, this is likely to become ever more important. If a museum is threatened with closure Friends' organisations can make representations to the governing body and campaign in a way which museum staff cannot.

Holding archaeological objects and literally touching the past is exciting, but finding an object, which has been lost for hundreds of years, is a thrill. Excavation immediately springs to mind but this is an expensive, skilled and destructive method of exploring the past. Consequently, there are far fewer opportunities for taking part in digs than there once were. However, excavations where the non-professionals are welcome do still take place but are usually in the form of training, so participants have to pay. Other types of fieldwork can be just as rewarding, less physically demanding and free. Systematic walking over ploughed fields and picking up any made object is a relatively simple way of recording archaeological sites. Finds are washed, identified and plotted out and concentrations of artefacts indicate the presence of a site. Field walking also complements excavation in that it allows whole landscapes to be examined rather than just one restricted area. Information from these large-scale surveys can also be passed on to the local sites and Monuments Record. Should a destructive development ever affect the area, then the sites discovered will be avoided or recorded before they are damaged.

Metal detecting is another valuable method of exploring the past. Recovering metallic objects from disturbed topsoil identifies the probable location of archaeological sites in the same way as field walking. When the finds are reported, this again gives some protection to the area. Metal detectors can be a useful tool on excavations either in the preliminary stages, to identify areas of particular potential, or for recovering objects from spoil heaps. Even the most eagle-eyed excavator will miss some mud-encased artefacts.

Earthwork surveys are particularly useful in areas that are not ploughed. Recording the extent and form of 'humps and bumps' can allow the type of site to be identified or at least show that the features would have to be more fully investigated prior to development.

Re-enactment and living history societies are another method of actively exploring life in earlier times. These groups tend to focus on the day-to-day experience of ordinary people. This often necessitates in-depth research into how objects were made and used. Details of costume and dress accessories are particularly important. Some even go as far as to research the language and mannerisms of the period in question.

National organisations such as the Council for British Archaeology (CBA) promote the interests of archaeology. Regional groups within the CBA organise day schools and site visits for their members. They may also comment on planning applications or projects likely to have an impact on the archae-ology of their region. The CBA recognises the interest that children have in ancient times and co-ordinates the Young Archaeologists Club. This has many local branches across the country run by volunteers. Meetings and trips take place regularly, but the highlight of the year are National Archaeology Days when museums, archaeological sites and excavations stage a vast range of events specifically aimed at Young Archaeologists and their peers.

English Heritage has roles on a number of levels but not least in ensuring that the sites within its own care are available to as wide an audience as possible. To enhance their natural appeal, the Special Events Unit provides hundreds of activities a year.

Even for those not able to physically visit museums and places of historic interest, it is still possible to enjoy and support archaeology. Websites, in increasing numbers, are offered by museums, re-enactment groups and national organisations, and there are also e-mail discussion lists coverings specific areas of interest. Television companies have recognised the entertain-ment value of past cultures and civilisations. This has resulted in many excellent programmes, which are vital for raising the profile of our heritage.

Taking part in any of the activities mentioned above is rewarding in itself. However, it also demonstrates to national and local bodies that people value knowing about and preserving the past and considers it a resource worth passing on to future generations. Only if this case is made at every level, at every opportunity, will those in financial power support the institutions that we need to interpret and preserve our inheritance. Our past is fragile. We can protect it, or we will lose it. The choice is ours.

Bibliography

Alexander, M., *Beowulf, A Verse Translation,* Penguin Classics 1973

Alexander, M., *The Earliest English Poems,* Penguin Classics 1977

Allason-Jones, L., *Women in Roman Britain,* British Museum Publications 1989

Arnold, C. J., *The Anglo-Saxon Cemeteries of the Isle of Wight,* Trustees of the British Museum 1982

Bede, *A History of the English Church and People,* Penguin Classics 1968

Boyle, A., Jennings, D. & Miles, S., *The Anglo-Saxon Cemetery at Butler's Field Lechlade, Gloucestershire,* Oxford Archaeology Unit, Oxford University Committee for Archaeology 1998

Care-Evans, A., *The Sutton Hoo Ship Burial,* British Museum Publication 1986

Cook, A.M., *The Anglo-Saxon Cemetery at Fonaby,* Lincolnshire Occasional Papers in Lincolnshire History and Archaeology 6 1981

Cook, A.M. Dacre, M.W. *Excavations at Portway, Andover 1973-1975,* Oxford University Committee for Archaeology 1985

Croom, A., *Roman Clothing and Fashion,* Tempus 2000

Dark, K., *Britain and the End of The Roman Empire,* Tempus 2000

Evison, V, *An Anglo-Saxon Cemetery at Great Chesterford, Essex* CBA 1994

Evison, V. & Hill, P., *Two Anglo-Saxon Cemeteries at Beckford, Hereford and Worcester,* CBA 1996

Green, B. & Rogerson, A., *The Anglo-Saxon Cemetery at Bergh Apton, Norfolk: Catalogue* East Anglian Archaeology 7, Norfolk Archaeological Unit 1978

Green, B., Rogerson, A. & White, S.G., *Morning Thorpe Anglo-Saxon Cemetery Norfolk,* East Anglian Archaeology 36 Norfolk Museums Service 1987

Hagen, A., *A Handbook of Anglo-Saxon Food: Processing and Consumption,* Anglo-Saxon Books 1992

Hagen, A., *A Second Handbook of Anglo-Saxon Food and Drink: Production and Distribution,* Anglo-Saxon Books 1995

Hamerow, H., *Excavations at Mucking Volume 2: The Anglo-Saxon Settlement,* English Heritage in Association with British Museum Press 1993

Hamerow, H. & Pickin, J., 'An Early Anglo-Saxon Cemetery At Andrew's Hill, Easington, County Durham', *Durham Archaeological Journal 11* 1995

Haughton, C. & Powlesland, D., *West Heslerton, The Anglian Cemetery,* The Landscape Research Centre Limited 1999

Herbert, K., *Looking for the Lost Gods of England,* Anglo-Saxon Books 1994

Hills, C., *The Anglo-Saxon Cemetery at Spong Hill, North Elmham Part I*, East Anglian Archaeology Report 6 Norfolk Archaeological Unit 1977

Hills, C. & Penn, K., *Spong Hill Part II*, East Anglian Archaeology Report No. 11 Norfolk Archaeological Unit

Hines, J., *The Scandinavian Character of Anglian England in the pre-Viking Period*, BAR British Series 124 1984

Hinton, A., *A Smith in Lindsey: The Anglo-Saxon Grave at Tattershall Thorpe, Lincolnshire*, The Society for Medieval Archaeology 2000

Hirst, S., *An Anglo-Saxon Inhumation Cemetery at Sewerby, East Yorkshire*, York University Archaeological Publications 1985

Hodges, H., *Artifacts: An Introduction to Early Materials and Technology*, John Baker 1976

Hooke, D., *Landscape of Anglo-Saxon England*, Leicester University Press 1998

Hutton, R., *The Pagan Religions of the Ancient British Isles*, BCA 1991

Johnson, S., *Later Roman Britain*, Paladin 1980

Kinsley, G.A., *Broughton Lodge*, University of Nottingham 1993

Liddle, P., Glasswell, S. & Cooper, N., 'Empingham I Early Anglo-Saxon Settlement and Cemetery' in Cooper, N., *The Archaeology of Rutland Water Leicestershire Archaeology Monograph No. 6* 2000

Malim, T. & Hines, J., *The Anglo-Saxon Cemetery at Edix Hill (Barrington A) Cambridgeshire)*, CBA 1998

Meaney, A., *Anglo-Saxon Amulets and Curing Stones*, BAR British Series 1981

McKinley, J.I., *Spong Hill: Part VIII The Cremations*, East Anglian Archaeology 69 Norfolk Museum Service 1994

Myres, J. N. L., *A Corpus of Anglo-Saxon Pottery of the Pagan Period* Cambridge University Press 1977

Myres, J.N.L. & Green, B., *The Anglo-Saxon Cemeteries of Caistor-by-Norwich and Markshall Norfolk*, The Society of Antiquaries of London 1973

Owen, G.R., *Rites and Religions of the Anglo-Saxons*, David and Charles 1981

Owen-Crocker, G.R., *Dress in Anglo-Saxon England*, Manchester University Press 1986

Pollington, S., *Leechcraft: Early English Charms, Plantlore and Healing*, Anglo-Saxon Books 2000

Prag, J. & Neave, R., *Making Faces using Forensic and Archaeological Evidence*, British Museum Press 1997

Rackham, O., *Trees and Woodland in the British Landscape*, Phoenix 1990

Rickett, R., *Spong Hill: Part VIII The Iron Age, Roman and Early Saxon Settlement* East Anglian Archaeology 73 Norfolk Museums Service 1995

Sherlock, S.J., & Welch Martin, G., *An Anglo-Saxon Cemetery at Norton, Cleveland*, CBA 1992

Timby, J., *The Anglo-Saxon Cemetery at Empingham II, Rutland*, Oxbow Monograph 70 1996

Underwood, R., *Anglo-Saxon Weapons and Warfare*, Tempus 1999

Werner, J., 'Frankish Royal Tombs in the Cathedrals of Cologne and Saint-

Denis' *Antiquity Volume 38* 1964

West, S., *West Stow The Anglo-Saxon Village,* East Anglian Archaeology Report 24 Suffolk County Planning Department 1985

West, S., *Westgarth Gardens Anglo-Saxon Cemetery Suffolk: Catalogue,* East Anglian Archaeology 1988

Williams, H., *Cemetery Burial Rites and the Early Anglo-Saxons,* Lecture at Burial in Early Medieval Britain Conference 1999

Williams, P.W,. *An Anglo-Saxon Cemetery at Thurmaston, Leicestershire,* Leicestershire Museums, Art Galleries and Records Service 1983

Index

Numbers in **bold** refer to figures